FOOD

HOW WE HUNT AND GATHER IT ▌ HOW WE GROW AND EAT IT ▌ HOW WE BUY AND SELL IT ▌ HOW WE PRESERVE AND WASTE IT ▌ AND ▌ HOW SOME HAVE TOO MUCH AND OTHERS HAVE TOO LITTLE OF IT

MILTON MELTZER

The Millbrook Press ▌ *Brookfield, Connecticut*

**For Hildy—
who gives me food for thought,
and food for love**

Library of Congress Cataloging-in-Publication Data
Meltzer, Milton, 1915–
Food / by Milton Meltzer; decorations by Sharon Lane Holm.
p. cm.
Includes bibliographical references and index.
Summary: Discusses the social, political, economic, and
gastronomic aspects of food in its many forms.
ISBN 0-7613-0354-5 (lib. bdg.)
1. Food—Juvenile literature. 2. Food—Social aspects—
Juvenile literature. 3. Food crops—Juvenile literature. 4. Food
supply—Juvenile literature. [1. Food. 2. Food habits.]
I. Holm, Sharon Lane, ill. II. Title.
TX355.M42   1998
641.3—dc21   98-5097   CIP   AC

Published by The Millbrook Press, Inc.
2 Old New Milford Road
Brookfield, Connecticut 06804

▮ C O N T E N T S ▮

▌FOREWORD▐

You've probably thought of food as simply the things you eat and drink every day. The orange juice, the banana with cereal, the scrambled eggs, the bread and butter, the chicken, the fish, the steak, the burger or hot dog, the ice cream, the candy, the dozens of other things you stuff into your mouth without a thought.

But who produced that food? Where did it come from? How did it get to your table? Why does it cost what it does? Is it good for you or bad for you? Will there be enough of it to feed you tomorrow and tomorrow and tomorrow? What if there isn't enough? Or what if you haven't the money to pay for it?

Unless we're lucky enough not to be starving, food is something we take for granted. Yet without it, where would we be? I don't mean just you and me. I mean everybody, everybody in the whole wide world.

Without food, there would be no human beings and no history.

Food is humankind's most basic need. Ever since our species appeared on this planet, nothing has concerned us more.

No one who tries to write the history of the everyday lives of the billions of men and women who have come before us can ignore the quest for food. The knowledge of how our ancestors dealt with the production of food, its distribution, and its consumption, opens the door to understanding food in our own time.

And it may also give us ideas about what we need to do to prevent the acute shortage of food that threatens the world in the 21st century.

Food and the search for it has been a powerful force in shaping the world's and our own history. It has had a great influence on population and its growth or decline, on the rise of cities, on the expansion of trade, on economic and political thought, on class differences, on wars and revolutions, on discovery and exploration, on religion and science . . .

To sketch that history in all those aspects would be impossible in a book this size. So I'll try to focus on broad developments and principles and to provide some useful details and examples to illustrate key points.

As I did my research, I came across many incidents, personalities, and odd facts that intrigued me. Now and then these punctuate the story to give you the flavor of what I found and to share the pleasure of discovery.

Milton Meltzer

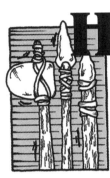How humans lived before the discovery of agriculture

Look about you at the way most people get their food nowadays. They go into the neighborhood grocery store or supermarket and buy whatever they need (if they can afford it): fresh fruits and vegetables, dairy products, meat, fish, frozen foods, packaged goodies. They are exchanging the money they earn for the products of other people's labor.

It wasn't always like this. For about 98 percent of human time on this planet, people caught or collected what food nature happened to provide. For most of the time until modern humans (*Homo sapiens*) evolved, 200,000 to 100,000 years ago, all people on Earth fed themselves only by hunting wild animals, fishing, and gathering wild plants.

Their food was mostly vegetable materials—nuts and roots and seeds, whatever they could find. To a small degree they hunted animals. It was often insects and frogs and lizards and snakes—small animals. For it was a lot harder to capture the big ones, like a buffalo or a rhinoceros.

Not an easy way to live, as only a small fraction of wild plants and animals are edible—or worth hunting or gathering. Most species are useless as food because they are indigestible, poisonous, have little nutritional value, are hard to gather and prepare, or dangerous to hunt.

Premodern humans, who lived in the early Stone Age, were believed to be only scavengers of meat and foragers of plants. But startling new evidence of early Stone Age ancestors suggests that they had skills and resourcefulness once thought to be true only of fully modern humans. In Germany in 1997, archaeologists excavated three complete wooden spears they said were carved about 400,000 years ago. Each one, 6 feet (1.8 meters) long and 2 inches (5 centimeters) in diameter, with a sharp tip, was carved from the trunk of a spruce tree. The scientists believe these are the oldest complete hunting weapons so far discovered to have been used by humans.

Found together with stone tools and the butchered remains of more than ten horses, these ancient spears must have been hurled not at such small animals as squirrels but at much larger game. The scientists concluded that systematic hunting went on that long ago, with foresight and planning and the use of the right technology.

Life was short in those prehistoric times. Few lived beyond the age of 40; many died before reaching 20. Often the weather or the landscape was not hospitable. You could be the victim of extreme cold, vitamin deficiencies, food poisoning, or seasonal malnutrition. In some regions you were dependent on a single animal—the reindeer, the caribou, the bison—and had to arrange your life around the habits of that creature. People preferred to eat meat when they could hunt animals, for that provided more sustenance for more people than any other kind of food.

At the end of the last Ice Age, around 11,000 B.C., most people lived in bands, tiny societies of 5 to 80 people, closely related by birth or marriage. The bands had no permanent single base of residence. Nor did they have formal institutions such as government and laws.

Everyone who was physically able foraged for food. Hunting seems to have been done mostly by men and boys. After the kill, the hunters carved up the carcass, discarding most of the bones and waste material, and carried the usable meat back to the cave or campsite. If near a river, people used a club or spear to kill the larger fish and trapped smaller ones by damming the water with upright stakes or laced branches. If near a seacoast, they could collect shellfish. Eventually fishermen invented fishhooks of various kinds as well as the harpoon, fishing nets, and the bow and arrow. Catching quantities of fish off the coast had to wait until the dugout canoe and reed raft were developed and oars perfected.

While the men in the band hunted, women's work was to collect whatever food material was nearby. It could include such small animals as snails and little turtles as well as edible roots, grasses, acorns, nuts, and berries, depending on the season and the band's location.

Gathering required patience and persistence, unlike hunting, which was sporadic. But the gathering of food was no less important. For hunting was sometimes poor, and everyone depended on what the women gathered.

It was a hard life.

 ## How farming was "invented"

What made life less hard was the "invention" of farming. The archaeologists who dig into ancient ruins believe farming began about 12,000 years ago. That's only the thinnest sliver of time seen against the seven million years humans have existed. "The adoption of agriculture," says the historian Norman Davies, "was the most fundamental change in human history. It created the first form of artificial habitat—the cultivated countryside."

Farming, put simply, is the investment of human labor to assist the growth of plants and animals. For the most part that labor has been devoted to promoting crops—especially cereals and tubers—that would produce a lot of calories and could then be stored.

How do we know where farming began—and when? The best evidence comes from the identification of plant and animal remains uncovered by archaeologists. Using radiocarbon dating of materials uncovered at a dig, as well as other methods of technological analysis, they can estimate when and where food production developed. It is now believed that the domestication of crops and ani-

11

mals arose altogether independently in at least five areas of the Earth, and possibly nine. That is, people in those areas developed farming on their own, without being influenced by the introduction of crops or animals from other places.

The five areas where food production originated, according to scientist Jared Diamond, were the ancient Middle East (Iraq), China, Mesoamerica (Mexico and neighboring parts of Central America), the Andes of South America, and the eastern United States. In addition, food production probably arose in three areas of Africa (the Sahel zone, tropical West Africa, and Ethiopia), and in New Guinea.

How could this have come about? After millions of years of gathering fruits and vegetables, people discovered that they could actively influence the growth of plants. Someone dropped some seeds by chance one fall, and the next spring found grain growing where the seeds had fallen. And then, by a great mental leap, connected the two events. It happened, we now know, between about 8500 B.C. and 2500 B.C.

It should be clear that the first farming began not by anyone's conscious choice. No one had ever seen farming before, so how could they know what it was like? Rather, it evolved by people making keen observations: A seed fell, then a plant grew. Do *this?* And then maybe *that* will happen? Early experiments in agriculture may have begun in some such way. Seeds were buried, stored in caves, or set aside in specially built shelters to preserve them for the next growing season.

People observed and drew the right conclusions. So they scratched seeds into the earth and came back a few months later to harvest what was there. Whatever insects and weeds and disease had not taken, these first farmers got. How much? Certainly more than they had found before.

It was in the Middle East that the earliest definite dates for both plant (8500 B.C.) and animal (8000 B.C.) domestication occurred. That region, once known as the Fertile Crescent, later was called Mesopotamia. Today it is the country of Iraq. The first plants domesticated were wheat, peas, and olives, and the first animals, sheep and goats.

In other areas of the world farmers learned to raise different crops: rice, millet, corn, beans, squash, potatoes, yams, and sugarcane. And as for animals tamed—turkeys, llamas, guinea fowl, and silkworms.

The first fruit and nut trees marked the next stage of crop development, around 4000 B.C. These products included: olives, figs, dates, pomegranates, and grapes. Later came fruit trees that were harder to cultivate: apples, pears, plums, and cherries. Around the same time, needing much less effort, came plants that initially were pesky weeds in fields of cultivated crops. Transformed by the farmers from weeds to edibles, the community added rye and oats, turnips and radishes, beets and leeks, and lettuce to its diet.

When the first farmers began to grow grain the crop not only fed themselves but small animals that liked to eat the same food. What to do to protect their food supply? One way was to domesticate the animals preying on their fields. It was rather easy to do this with the wild sheep and goat, for both liked to hang out together and were quick to breed.

The goat's browsing habits helped the farmer clear the scrub away so he could cultivate more land. About 2,000 years after the taming of the goat and sheep, it was the pig's turn. Because pigs can't digest straw, grass, leaves, or twigs, they were no threat to the fields. But since they like the same food as humans, pig farming didn't arise until farmers could produce enough surplus to take care of the pig's needs.

The cow was the last major food animal to be domesticated. This happened around 6000 B.C.

Farmers learned they could get more than meat out of their tamed animals. Goats provided waterproof hair and skin, useful to make water bags. From sheep came wool and lots of fat for cooking and medicinal salves. The pig's lard and its skin were put to good use. Several uses were found for the tough, strong hide of the cow, while its dung provided fuel for the fire.

Not until some time later did farmers learn to use goats, sheep, and oxen for agricultural labor. The animals could tread seeds into the earth, pull a plow (when it was invented), and thresh the grain. Farmers added to their own muscle the strength of animals. The community had its first power tools.

■ ■ ■

How dogs were domesticated

Dogs are almost universally popular pets. Who would think of eating them? Yet breeds of dogs were developed and raised for food in Aztec Mexico, Polynesia, and ancient China. However, in human societies sometimes lacking in meat, dogs as a regular diet were a last resort. The Aztecs had no other domestic mammal. In Polynesia and ancient China there wasn't much choice for meat: It was pigs or dogs. In some parts of Southeast Asia today dog meat is considered a rare delicacy. The dogs that the Aztecs and Polynesians raised specifically for food were fattened on vegetables and garbage.

When Europeans settled in Tasmania, a large island region near Australia, they brought along dogs. The aboriginal Tasmanians had never seen dogs before. They began to raise them in large numbers for use in hunting. In Australia the wild dog, called the dingo, entered around 1500 B.C. Native Australians kept captive dingos as companions and watchdogs, and they even used them as "living blankets" on very cold nights. But never for food or for hunting.

Dogs are among the earliest domesticated wild animals. They first appear in the fossil record about 12,000 years ago. They are descended from Asian wolves, yet in physique and behavior are very different from them. Some dogs, like the Great Dane, are much bigger, while others, like the Pekingese, are much smaller. Think how different greyhounds and dachshunds are from each other and their ancestor. It's hard to believe the wolf was the common ancestor of all the varieties of dogs we now know.

The early wolf dogs had a cooperative connection with our ancient ancestors. In return for protection, food, and warmth, the dogs helped in hunting and tracking. They were used too as sentinels, pets, or food. But wild animals did not become domesticated merely because humans wanted to use them for whatever purpose. No, the animals had certain characteristics that lent themselves to partnership with people. The animals had to be willing to go along, willing to live with people. And many, actually most, wild animals are not like that. So they have never been domesticated.

How Jason won the Golden Fleece

Perhaps you've heard of the legend of the Golden Fleece. It's linked to the domestication of sheep. In ancient times the finest fleeced sheep were developed in Asia Minor and exported to the Mediterranean region. In Greek myth, Jason, the son of a king, sails with his crew of Argonauts to Colchis, a kingdom at the east end of the Black Sea, to obtain the Golden Fleece. It was considered an impossible task, for the sheep had magical powers and was guarded by a gigantic serpent. To gain the Golden Fleece, Jason had to yoke fire-breathing oxen, plow a field with them, sow the teeth of a dragon, and kill the armed men who sprang up. How Jason met the challenge and his fate thereafter is told in classical Greek poems and plays. Perhaps the wool-producing breeds of sheep we now have are descended in some way from the Golden Fleece.

How villages evolved into cities

Farming had obvious advantages over hunting and gathering. By concentrating on the species of plants and animals they could eat, the community got far more edible calories from their land. One acre (.4 hectare) could now feed 10 to 100 times more farmers and herders than hunter-gatherers were able to do.

The livestock fed more people by supplying meat and milk, and their manure, applied as fertilizer, greatly increased crop yields. With the larger domestic animals—such as the cow, horse, and water buffalo—pulling plows, more land could be tilled more easily than before.

Improved production of food had a profound effect in other ways. It led to the rise of civilization. Hunter-gatherers had to move around a lot to find wild plants and game. But farmers must stay close to their fields and animals, living in fixed communities. In turn that led to larger populations. Mothers no longer had to tote babies and small children as the tribe constantly roved for food. Staying in the village, they could bear and raise as many children as they could feed. A higher birthrate meant far more people living in settled communities.

If the community was staying put, then it could store the food surplus and protect it. With a surplus on hand, not everybody in the village had to be occupied with production of food. Enough was on hand to enable people to become full-time specialists—chiefs or kings, for instance, together with helpers to carry out orders. The political elite took control of food produced by others, levied taxes (paid in foodstuffs) to support their bureaucracy, and had ample time to politic. Crop surplus supported the expansion of long-distance trade and the merchants to carry it on.

In the small agricultural societies, chieftains rose to the top, sometimes inheriting leadership, sometimes winning it by their strength and achievements. In the larger societies, kingdoms developed. As these grew ever more complex, they carried out wars of conquest. That required soldiers, and the stored food supplies also fed this group of specialists. So too did the surplus support priests, artisans such as metalworkers who developed weapons and tools, crafts persons in textiles and ceramics, and scribes who recorded the deeds of kings and warriors.

As the number of people grew, farm villages evolved into cities. The rise of cities went along with such transforming innovations as writing, animals for traction, wheeled carts, metallurgy, craft specialization, and irrigation.

How more than food came out of farming

The giant step toward domestication of plants and animals turned out to have many important values other than the provision of food. Take clothing, blankets, nets, rope. They were made of natural fibers taken from crops and livestock. Going beyond raising crops for food, farmers ventured into fiber crops: cotton, the flax that linen comes from, and hemp. Woolen clothing comes from several domestic animals: sheep, goats, llamas, alpaca. Silk blouses, shirts, ties, stockings? From the cultivation of silkworms. Your leather shoes? From the hides of cows. Wasting very little, prehistoric people used the bones of domestic animals to create artifacts.

How time is telescoped

If farming is a "recent" development, just how recent do we mean? To get some idea of the scale of time, consider the history of the planet Earth as divided into six days of creation, each 666 million years long. On this scale, dinosaurs appear at 4:00 P.M. on the last day, and have disappeared by 9:00 P.M. on that day. Humans enter the story 3 minutes before midnight on the last day. And domestication of plants and animals begins on the tiniest fraction of a second of the last hour of that final day.

Not very long ago!

How good nutrition maintains our health

We eat to take in the nutrients our body needs. For proper nutrition we require all the essential nutrients: carbohydrates, fats, protein, vitamins, minerals, and water—and in the right balance to maintain our health and well-being.

Good nutrition helps the normal development and functioning of the body, as well as normal reproduction, growth, and maintenance. We cannot work steadily or efficiently without it, nor can we resist infection and disease. If we suffer damage or injury, nutrition helps to repair the body.

Each of the necessary nutrients has to be eaten in certain quantities and must be absorbed by the body from the intestine and used successfully. Many of these can be stored only briefly in the body; nature provides the mechanisms to excrete most of them.

Luckily the human body is well designed to avoid toxic food: It tends to taste bitter or sour. And designed as well to be attracted to the calories we need: They commonly taste sweet. We tend to store the scarce nutrients and to excrete the excess.

Our own behavior usually determines whether we get adequate nutrition. We can change food habits, and our activities may also have effects, changing our bodily needs or affecting the rate at which we absorb nutrients through the intestine or excrete them. Remember too that sometimes we have limited resources. Decisions affecting our health don't take place in a vacuum. Culture and custom, varying widely throughout the world, often present risks to good nutrition, which people take on because of tradition or fear to go against social pressure, much as young people continue to smoke tobacco despite the overwhelming evidence that it is harmful to their health.

And then, in just about every nation, there is the ever-present lack of means, often for many millions, to obtain the food that good nutrition requires. Poverty, unemployment, and low wages mean hunger, and acute hunger brings on famine, starvation, and death.

How life on Earth depends on water

Our two most precious resources are soil and water. All life on Earth depends on them. Sensible management of both is necessary for any community to thrive. Yet from the earliest societies on down, humans began to do harm to their environment by degrading both resources. In our own time, human abuse of the environment has grown worse, bringing us to the point of crisis.

Soil and water function together in the biosphere. The material basis of life is soil, and water is its essence. Almost all peoples seem to sense that. In many countries, rivers and springs are held sacred—the Nile, the Ganges, the Jordan. In many religions, water is taken not only as a physical cleansing agent but as a source of spiritual purification and renewal.

In our solar system, Earth is the only planet where water is abundant in liquid form. It is the liquid that supports active life. Geologists say that the population limit of a region is determined by how available water is. How much of it does a person need to subsist? How many people can the supply sustain? What could happen to affect the water supply?

People use water to drink and to cook, to grow food, domesticate aquatic and land animals, for forests and other cash crops, as well as for a great variety of other purposes. Agriculture is the major user of water. It accounts for about 70 percent of total withdrawals worldwide. About 17 percent of the world's cropland is irrigated, producing over a third of the harvest. (Industry is the second major user of water.) By the year 2000, it is predicted that an additional 25 to 30 percent more water will be needed to keep pace with the increase in agricultural land under irrigation.

The number of people water can support depends on how it is used or misused. For although Earth's stocks of water are immense, they are not limitless. Only a tiny portion of Earth's water—between 2 and 6 percent, it is estimated—is fresh. About 70 percent of that is locked in glaciers and permanent snow cover and aquifers more than a mile (1.6 kilometers) deep, much of it inaccessible. The other 30 percent is accessible groundwater.

Fresh water is perpetually recycled. It comes down from the sky as precipitation and goes back up again primarily as evaporation, and secondarily as transpiration. That is, the removal of water from the ground into plants and its evaporation from plants back to the atmosphere.

The local as well as regional supply of renewable fresh water varies widely from place to place, year to year, and seasonally within the year. Some areas get very heavy rainfall, others, very little. Often rivers and lakes are shared by more than one country, sometimes by several. The Danube in Europe touches more than a dozen countries. The Nile in Africa supplies eight countries before it reaches Egypt. Who has the right to use the water? It leads to constant argument over who gets what, when, and where.

Countries have been ranked for the least and greatest amount of the annual available fresh water per person. The result contrasts Djibouti (in Africa), with only 812 cubic feet (23 cubic meters) of fresh water per year, with Iceland, which has 29,000 times as much per person. Those are the extremes. The United States has about 349,614 cubic feet (9,900 cubic meters) per person per year.

Nature provides the water, but how much people can use it depends strongly on human investments made in cisterns, wells, dams, pipelines, and facilities for treatment and recycling of waste. As we will see in the chapter on irrigation (page 22), cisterns at least 2,000 years old have been found beneath every house and public building in the Negev desert of the Middle East. In the jungle of Guatemala, which has four rainy months a year, the Mayans built paved areas in the city of Tikal to catch fresh water during the city's rainy season of eight months, while a system of reservoirs watered homes and farms the year round.

Reservoirs today can contain globally twice the stock of water in all the world's rivers. San Francisco gets water from the distant Sierra Nevada Mountains, while New York City water comes from a far-flung network of reservoirs and aqueducts.

Wasteful use of water is common in most countries today. Affluent households often use more than 264 gallons (1,000 liters) per day per person. But in developing countries the use seldom goes above 13 gallons (50 liters) per person. In arid regions women walk several miles each day to fetch water for their families, carrying it in earthen jars or tin cans on their heads, and their use per person is close to the biological minimum of 0.5 to 1.3 gallons (2 to 5 liters) per day.

The quantity of water available matters much, but its quality is just as important. What physical, chemical, and biological agents are in the water? What is being done to manage discharged water? If water is contaminated it can be ruinous to human health. Until the early 20th century, and even later, just about everyone used unhealthy water. Today nearly half the people in the world suffer from diseases related to lack of water or contaminated water. Water-borne and food-borne diarrheal diseases endanger two billion people. These diseases account for the deaths of over three million people each year, almost all of them children.

Most of the trouble occurs in developing countries, and most of the victims are poor. In the Third World's impoverished lands, water is often a deadly drink. A dispatch from India reports the case of a young mother living in a slum who serves unboiled water to her 5- and 7-year-old boys in her one-room hovel. The water has already killed two of her children, a 15-month-old boy and a 7-month-old girl. But everyone in the slum drinks the water, usually without boiling it. To boil water consistently would cost about four dollars a month in kerosene, almost a third of the mother's earnings as a housemaid. If she spent the money on that, she'd have less for food.

The water comes from a pipe that runs into the slum. The pipes are cracked and pass through a ditch filled with sewage. Even if the water were properly heated at its source, sewage would seep into the water to produce the most deadly sickness in today's world—diarrhea.

Few realize that cattle are a major source of pollution of water. Cattle produce about one billion tons of organic wastes each year. Much of it, in the United States, runs off into the groundwater and surface water. It contaminates wells, rivers, streams, and lakes throughout the country. One scientist estimates that the amount of pollution from cattle and other livestock is double the amount from all U.S. industrial sources.

United Nations experts say the most fundamental health challenge in the world at the end of the 20th century may be the same as it apparently was four thousand years ago—sanitation. Nothing would make a greater difference in the life of the Indian mother's family than clean water and a toilet. One of the most persistent reasons for poor hygiene is simply that there is almost no water to wash with in many parts of Africa, India, and China.

It's not the total amount of freshwater supplies that is the chief barrier to satisfying people's needs for water. Rather, it is the variation in location and amount. If the vast excesses of fresh water available in some regions could be diverted to meet requirements elsewhere, the problem could be solved. But how to get the right amounts of water to the right places at the right time? And get the most use from that fresh water?

If population growth continues, present water shortages could become worse in many regions. The range of choice about how to use the available fresh water will be reduced. What could postpone water shortages? Improvements in recycling, pricing, and the efficiency of delivering and using water, say the experts.

How irrigation creates civilizations

Irrigation?

Without that close bond between soil and water, farming is impossible. An effective soil-water system has determined the long-range life span of many civilizations. The earliest farmers found that after only a few years of cultivation, soil became exhausted. And it could take several decades for it to regenerate. To clear the land for planting, farmers stripped away trees and scrub, and when the land was overworked, it soon turned to desert.

You can see what might happen in the story of a people called the Sumerians. They lived around 5000 B.C. at the head of the Persian Gulf. Sumer was a flat, brown plain, dry and dusty, swept by desert winds or deluged periodically by sudden overflows of the Tigris and Euphrates rivers. The Sumerians gradually transformed their difficult region from a seasonally parched plain into a land of broad grain and forage fields and date-palm plantations. How did they do it? By figuring out a way to water their fields. They dug passages in the banks of streams so that the water flowed out into narrow canals, and they built dikes to control the flow.

The canals served too as waterways and fish ponds. They irrigated grainfields, palm groves, and grasslands, which supplied feed for sheep and cattle. Better, richer crops were harvested than ever before. Some historians say 30 times as much. And they had the surplus to trade for the raw materials their own land lacked, such as building stones, metals, and gems.

As methods of irrigation improved, and the surplus of food mounted, it took specialists to look after the maintenance of ditches and canals and to see that people got their fair share of the water. Meanwhile, Sumer's small mud settlements were replaced by brick homes and temples. A city was born out of the planned achievement of combining land and water.

Soon other city-states followed—in the Nile Valley, the Indus valley, Asia, Mesoamerica, and South America . . .

How to survive in a desert

What about farming in the desert? Could it be done?

A desert is an arid region, usually partly covered with sand. It has little or no vegetation, and can support only limited and specially adapted animal life.

There are both cold deserts and warm deserts. The cold regions—about one sixth of the Earth's surface—are often covered perpetually by snow or ice. The warm deserts—about one fifth of the world's land surface—may have no rain for periods of several years. The largest of the warm deserts lie about 20° and 30° north and south of the equator. When an area has an annual rainfall of 10 inches or less, it is rated as a desert.

The people of the ancient world saw the desert as a unique world, something very separate and very different from the seas and the habitable lands. They felt the desert was awesome, terrifying, dangerous—and useless. The Bible speaks of the desert as "the land unsown." To survive in a desert you had to be ingenious, devising ways to get supplies of water either by extracting it from underground aquifers (if they existed) or by bringing it in somehow from elsewhere. Only by such inventive schemes could agriculture be possible, even if limited to quite small areas.

Yet some desert regions were made liveable by marvelously inventive and hardworking people. Proof of it can be traced in the records of such civilizations in North Africa, in Jordan, in the Negev region of southern Israel, and in the American Southwest.

These desert regions are extremely arid, with too little rainfall to sustain crops. It's almost impossible to graze animals there. Yet in the deserts of Judea and the Negev, the Israelites, beginning around 1200 B.C., established villages, fortresses, and trade routes. For the indispensable water, they carved cisterns out of the rock to hold whatever precious rain might fall.

After the kingdom of Judah was destroyed by the Babylonians, and the Jews were removed, another people settled in the Negev and, mastering the problems of desert life, created a great civilization. These were the Nabataeans. Nomadic traders at first, they eventually produced architects and engineers, as well as expert hydrologists and farmers. Their domain lay across ancient trade routes. Caravans passing through the desert needed water and food, and the Nabataeans established bases along the main routes, offering sources of water and provisions. As the local populations grew, these bases evolved into self-supporting villages and then into cities.

Underpinning this growth was agriculture. If not for farming, the population of tens of thousands could not have been sustained. The Nabataeans too created great cisterns and built dikes. The major source of water in that region could only be the collection of surface runoff obtained from sloping ground during the winter rains. They stored the water in their cisterns, doling it out when needed to people and livestock. This type of agriculture, called runoff farming, was applied to their small farm plots, which they leveled off and terraced to obtain the desired amount of water as well as to conserve both soil and water.

The agricultural methods of the ancient Nabataeans were much like those evolved by a quite different civilization, far removed in space and time. The Anasazi, or Pueblo Indians, of the American Southwest contended with much the same conditions in their environment. Their culture began to develop around A.D. 100 in the region where the borders of four states intersect: Arizona, New Mexico, Colorado, and Utah.

At first hunter-gatherers, the Anasazi added to their diet by growing maize, pumpkins, and beans. Later they quit hunting and gathering to work exclusively as farmers. To gather and conserve water in their arid region they developed the same kind of runoff system that the ancient people of the Negev had used. The community planned a way to control surface water, which showed a great talent for engineering. Dams, reservoirs, canals, and ditches channeled runoff water to terraces and fields. So effective was their system that it led to a rise in population and the enrichment of their cultural life.

The Anasazi civilization flourished for over a thousand years. In the 12th century it began to decline—for reasons no one can be sure of. Their great cliff homes, storage pits, and ceremonial chambers were abandoned. Although several possible causes of this strange collapse of a culture have been offered, scientists think the most probable is what threatens to doom people in arid regions—a severe, prolonged drought. Paleoecological research indicates that the whole region was blighted by a drought that persisted for about sixty years, from A.D. 1130 to 1190.

Yes, both the Nabataean and the Anasazi civilizations declined. It's clear, however, that the innovative methods they devised to obtain water for their farming are just as valid today for arid regions wherever they may be.

How the Nile nourishes Egypt

The Earth's greatest oasis is the green valley of the Nile. The world's largest river, the Nile runs more than 4,000 miles (6,436 kilometers) from its remotest headstream in Central Africa to its delta on the Mediterranean Sea. A vast contrast is seen between the dark fertile soil watered by the Nile and the forbidding Sahara Desert that lies just beyond its banks and stretches all across North Africa.

For over 5,000 years the Nile valley has nourished Egyptian civilization. Like Mesopotamia, which developed somewhat earlier, Egyptian civilization has depended almost entirely on irrigated agriculture. The Nile's gift to Egypt is both water and silt. The farmland of the delta, which contains 60 percent of the cultivated lands, is built out of deposits laid down by the Nile in flood time. The fertile silt from the highlands of Ethiopia adds nutrients to the land and nourishes its crops.

Back around 5200 B.C., Egypt's early farmers learned to tame the unregulated floods to water the banks of the river. When a flood receded, they would cast their seeds in the mud. If a weak flood failed to soak the soil, crops failed and famine set in.

The solution? Farmers figured out that dikes built across their plot of ground would create basins to hold enough water to soak into the earth so that it could sustain the roots of crops during the growing season. At times, if too much water flooded in, the farmers breached their dikes to let the surplus run out.

Egypt's farmers—the peasants—became so productive that their surplus crops fed the country's specialists: artisans, merchants, scribes, noblemen, priests, officials, and, towering over all, the pharaohs, rulers of Egypt. The pharaoh and his queen were worshiped as divine beings. Far below them, at the bottom of society, were the great mass of peasants. Technically free, they lived almost like serfs. They worked the lands of the pharaoh, the temples, or the nobles on a sharecropping system. They could not be sold, and they owned their homes, so they were not slaves. But they were still bound to the land. If the land was sold, the peasants went along with it to serve the new owners.

The peasants were exempted from military service because they were needed on the land. But they were drafted between farming seasons to build the massive pyramids, which house the pharaohs' tombs. One of these alone, the great pyramid at Giza, was made of 2,300,000 stone blocks, weighing about two and a half tons each. The Greek historian Herodotus said it took 100,000 peasant workers 20 years to build the pyramid.

The records of ancient Egypt that have survived—written on papyrus or painted on walls—reveal an agriculture very much like the farming of Egyptian people today. In modern times too Egypt has suffered famines such as the seven lean years predicted by Joseph in the Bible.

But the economic level of ancient Egypt is not what Egypt knows now. Experts believe that Egypt's population in the time of the pharaohs was about 2 million. Today, however, Egypt's population numbers more than 60 million, which means that 30 times as many people as in the ancient era are now struggling to survive on the same farmland and with the same resource of water.

Thousands of years ago Egypt was able to produce enough surplus food to sustain other peoples in need. Often the huge Roman Empire had to buy, trade, or loot Egypt's surplus to feed its peoples. Now, however, Egypt imports one half of the food it needs to feed its own huge population. And the soil it once could rely on to meet its needs is rapidly deteriorating.

How the partnership between humans and horses began

Millions of years ago the only way people could move long distances on land was to walk. To transport goods you had to carry the load on your back. Domestication of animals changed all that. At last you could move not only people but heavy goods without human labor—and do it rapidly and over long distances. Domestic animals became the main means of land transportation.

Depending on what part of the world you were in, you had the horse, the donkey, the yak, the reindeer, the llama, or the camel to help you. People rode them or used them to carry packs. Cows and horses pulled wagons; reindeer pulled sleds.

The horse we know today evolved from ancestors that predated humans by about 60 million years. Their fossilized skeletons have been dug up in North America and northern Europe. The modern horse—Equus—arrived around 2.5 million years ago, spreading from the plains of North America and South America and across the land bridge from Alaska to Siberia and all parts of Eurasia. (Later, the horse disappeared from the Western Hemisphere, to return in the 15th century on the second voyage of Columbus.)

Wild horses were undoubtedly hunted for food. That was the first use of the animal by humans about 100,000 years ago. Not till about 3500 B.C. did some people discover that not only could the horse be eaten, it could be used alive. Domesticating the horse seems to have been done first in a region that is now Ukraine, at the eastern edge of the Eurasian steppes. These pastoral people rounded up the animals, used them for meat, for hides, and for milk from the mares. They learned to ride the horse and to yoke it to pull loads.

Horses became the main military power in ancient warfare. When hitched to battle chariots, the horse revolutionized warfare in the Near East, the Mediterranean region, and China. The animal enabled the small bands of Spanish conquistadors to overthrow the Aztec and Inca empires, and the Huns to sweep from the steppes of Asia over the vast Roman Empire. For thousands of years, down to World War I (1914–18), when trucks and tanks replaced them, the horse was the main vehicle for assault and transportation.

How the plow broke the plains

Irrigation was only one of the tools that helped the spread of agriculture in ancient times. The early farmers developed many ways to improve the yield of their plants—the ax, for one. It enabled them to girdle and cut down trees so that the sunlight needed to stimulate the growth of plants would reach the forest floor. The hoe, too, was an important tool for stirring the soil before seeding—as was the sickle, for harvesting matured grain.

The plow—first pictured in Sumer around 3000 B.C.—appeared in the river valleys of the Tigris and Euphrates and soon after in Egypt and in China. The Sumerians developed yokes for harness animals and animal-drawn plows. Coupled to strong domesticated animals, the plow greatly increased the farmer's ability to produce an agricultural surplus from a variety of soils and under varying climatic conditions. To work his plow to best advantage the farmer needed a flat, smooth stretch of ground, for the plow couldn't be easily turned or adjusted to irregular surfaces. It took a good part of the farmer's labor to extend his fields, and it made a lasting change in the landscape.

So both plant and animal domestication became even more tightly linked through the plow. The farmer had to take care of the animals he needed to draw the plow and the crops he needed to feed the animals. Yet, looked at from a much longer time perspective, the plow also did great damage. For by pulverizing the soil and weakening its cover of plants, the plow opened the way to erosion by wind and water.

One of the most notorious examples of erosion occurred in the 1930s in America's Great Plains region. During and after World War I, through a belt of over a hundred counties, starting in Kansas and running into Texas, farmers lured by quick profits had plowed submarginal land. Ample rainfall for a few decades had produced rich crops of wheat, but the rains stopped eventually and a terrible dryness set in. Late in 1931 a series of disastrous droughts and dust storms began. The topsoil blew away in huge clouds, darkening the skies, burying everything from houses and barns to fences and machinery. The "black blizzard" cost the nation hundreds of millions of tons of soil and desolated thousands of families in the Great Plains states. They took to the roads. Within the next five years, 350,000 Dust Bowl farmers deserted the homesteads they or their pioneer ancestors had thought to root themselves in forever and headed for California.

The Dust Bowl calamity, popularized in John Steinbeck's novel *The Grapes of Wrath* and then in both a film and a play, has been repeated on just as great a scale in such regions as the Sahel in sub-Saharan Africa. Called "desertification," it occurs when the plowing of a semiarid region denudes it of vegetation, with uncontrolled erosion following.

■ ■ ■

How a crumb of soil banks billions of organisms

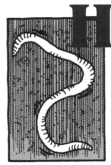

If someone builds a road through your suburb, paves a street in your village, or erects a skyscraper in your city, they have to scrape away topsoil. Soil is the place where plants put down their roots. It's also home to an incredible variety of valuable microorganisms that are the workers in nature's "underground economy." As Lester Brown, head of the scientific research team at Worldwatch, puts it, "Insects, worms and microorganisms provide the priceless service of decomposing organic material, making nutrients available to plants, controlling diseases, and improving the texture and water-holding capacity of soil. The tiny tunnels they dig provide space for air, water, and roots to move through the soil."

This stuff in the soil is alive. How alive? One scientist has come up with these estimates. Just a pinch, just a crumb of soil, he says, is home to 30,000 protozoa, 50,000 algae, 400,000 fungi, and billions of bacteria. Under a square yard (less than a square meter) of pasture you would find some 50,000 small earthworms, 50,000 insects and mites, and about 12 million roundworms. Altogether, in about 2.5 acres (1 hectare) of soil, you could expect there to be a ton of earthworms, a ton of arthropods, 331 pounds (150 kilograms) of protozoa, 331 pounds (150 kilograms) of algae, 3,748 pounds (1,700 kilograms) of bacteria and 5,952 pounds (2,700 kilograms) of fungi.

What's the use of all that stuff under our feet? These organisms decompose plants so that other plants can recycle and replace them. Without them there would be no oxygen, and without oxygen there would be no animal life of any kind—including us.

How long does it take for that topsoil to form? For just a tiny fraction of an inch (less than a centimeter) it takes between two hundred and one thousand years. Even when farmers do a good job of taking care of their land, the topsoil erodes 10 to 20 times faster than it is formed.

When that grunting and groaning bulldozer comes in to prepare the way for a road or a building, it scrapes away the whole mass of living stuff in minutes. Gone is some farmland.

Take Britain alone—a relatively small country, with figures of land loss easier to calculate. Graham Harvey, in a book called *The Killing of the Countryside*, reports that 97 percent of meadowland has gone since World War II. Since that time, 150,000 miles (241,401 kilometers) of hedgerow have been lost, at the rate of 11,000 miles (17,703 kilometers) a year. More than 200,000 farms have disappeared resulting in the loss of 880,000 jobs, or more than three out of four farmworkers.

As we'll see later, farmable land is disappearing all over the world with frightening speed.

How ancient agriculture used slave labor

In early hunting societies it was the practice to kill defeated enemies. There was no surplus food to feed captives and make use of their labor. But when farming or herding reached the stage where more was produced than needed to feed the family or community, it made the taking of slaves practicable. The loser in a conflict kept his life and in return was made to work, caring for the flocks or laboring in the fields.

Slave labor in agriculture goes back in history some ten thousand years. Archaeologists digging into the soil of ancient buried cities of the Near East have unearthed thousands of clay tablets recording the functions of slavery in Sumer, Babylon, and Assyria. The Egyptians of the time of the pharaohs took prisoners in their wars and enslaved them, but they were not needed for agricultural labor because there were so many peasants. Ancient Chinese art shows field slaves working under the whip of overseers. In early Greek culture of some 3,000 years ago, the people lived a simple farm life. Slavery was mild. Slaves were not treated like beasts of burden but as human beings sharing the family system of labor. But in the next several centuries, as Greeks planted colonies all along the Mediterranean and Black Sea shorelines, wars and slavery increased.

And so it went in country after country, century after century. It was always the same division of people—the free and the slave—regardless of color. People of every color enslaved one another. War itself became a good business because of profits from slavery.

In the Roman world, plantation slavery began in the second century B.C. Cheap slave labor made large holdings of farm and pasture profitable. The small plots of the peasants gave way to the large estates operated by slave labor for the absentee owners. Cattle ranches, vineyards, and olive groves were all manned by slaves. Ranches became so large their masters could not ride around them. Records show one agricultural estate was worked by 4,117 slaves.

While the great estates expanded, the small farms shrank, and free labor was supplanted by slave labor. The dispossessed peasants came to the cities for relief or wandered the countryside to seek work as hired hands during the harvest and vintage seasons.

While some Roman treatises on farming advised plantation owners to treat their slaves well, as the best way to get the most work out of them, others advocated the use of the whip and of chains for men doing gang labor. "Like worn-out tools, the aged slaves and the sick slaves" should be disposed of, advised another farming expert. And, he went on, let only the slave bailiff or foreman have a wife, for if all the males had their women, it would cost far too much, and besides, the children born to them, until they reached working age (if they should survive that long), would only add to the expense.

How people lived in the Middle Ages

What happened to the way people got their food in the Middle Ages? Those medieval centuries extended from the fall of the Roman Empire in the fifth century A.D. to the 1500s. To the question why the empire perished, many answers have been offered. No single factor was responsible. It was a complex of social, political, and economic problems that the empire's rulers could not or would not solve that led to the end of the ancient world.

The operation of the large estates of the empire continued into the Middle Ages, gradually evolving into the feudal system. Under it the great majority of the people lived on manors or estates.

A manor was a territorial unit—an estate belonging either to the king or to a lord or to the church, and containing a village of serfs. The lord had his home farm, and the rest of the land was occupied by his tenants. The serfs had to cultivate the land and couldn't leave it without the lord's permission. Nor could they sell an ox or marry without his consent. As rent, the serfs paid a stated amount of produce each year, and they also had to carry out specified tasks, including military service.

The lord held power over the community, but he had responsibilities too. He supplied military protection against enemies or invaders, the technical and legal skills of his agents, and the major facilities—mill, winepress, barns. The peasants supplied their labor, their animals, their tools, their produce.

Most of the peasants were not slaves, but they were not fully free either. The line between slave and serf, or slave and freeman, would be very hard to draw. For in feudal Europe there was no systematic regulation of rights and duties. Each manor had its own recognized customs, and those customs had the force of law. Nowhere, however, did the customs remain fixed. As conditions changed, so did the customs change. Famine, plague, war, invasion—all could force shifts in ways of living, introduce new customs, and change old ones.

The peasants produced the supply of food that sustained the nobles (who ruled), the priests (who ministered), and themselves. Everywhere in Europe the system was pretty much the same.

To work the land, the serfs at first had only the elementary tools: picks, spades, forks, rakes, scythes, sickles. There were horses and oxen, but the horse collar, the harness, and the stirrup would not be invented until about A.D. 900. With tandem hitching impossible, the peasants had to work even harder than their animals.

At no time did slavery vanish from feudal Europe. In the England of the Anglo-Saxon era, for example, slaves continued to be a factor in the rural economy. They tilled the farms alongside the freemen and the serfs, and almost all of this farm labor lived in great squalor. Their huts were a single windowless room, small and cramped, with the floor a refuse dump. There were no windows or shutters or chimney. People slept on their straw pallets, often without blankets. Some huts had no beds. There was an open hearth with the smoke from the fire worming its way out through a hole in the thatched roof. The house was usually built of wood.

Gradually in many parts of Europe the freemen of the lower classes and most of the slaves mingled in a new class—the serfs. Slaves were emancipated because it was to the advantage of their masters as the economy changed. The large farms of the past were subdivided, so masses of slaves were no longer needed. Greater wealth could be derived from the exaction of rents and services than from the operation of vast estates.

But rarely were slaves freed with no strings attached. Most freedmen were made responsible to their old masters or a new one (often the church) in whose care the master placed them. Such obligations were considered hereditary. This made the freedman the tenant of his patron. A yearly head tax levied on the freedman by the patron was common. So the former slave, now a serf, paid a price for the protection given him by the master who was now his patron. Thus serfdom grew.

It was not easy for the people of medieval Europe to feed themselves. Each village tried to produce all it needed for subsistence and to build up a reserve for the inevitable famine to come. But with a scanty labor force and poor techniques, it was hard going. And then the church took 10 percent of all animal and vegetable products, often passing it on to the local lord who had taken control of church revenue. Then too out of the peasant's labor came the food required to feed the military. And the meat-hungry lord grabbed for his own table the few head of cattle that could be spared from field labor and stock breeding.

Medieval monarchs and bishops were often on the road, making tours of inspection or just out for pleasure, and ready to accept a tribute or taxes in kind on the spot. They traveled with large retinues of courtiers or monks who had to be fed. The rural folk knew what was expected of them. In the eighth century when the king of Wessex stopped at an English village, the peasants turned over to him what they were legally bound to supply: 300 round loaves, 10 sheep, 10 geese, 20 chickens, 10 cheeses, 10 measures of honey, 5 salmon, and 100 eels. One French village in the ninth century was obliged to supply the local monastery, every week, with 100 loaves, 30 gallons (114 liters) of fat, or tallow, 32 gallons (121 liters) of wine, and 1 gallon (4 liters) of oil, as well as 60 gallons (227 liters) of ale a day.

How a new invention changed ways of working and living

Early in the Middle Ages, farming was revolutionized by a simple new tool—the moldboard plow. Plows themselves were not new. The Sumerians of the Fertile Crescent had used the "scratch" plow to turn the soil. But over the centuries it had been improved by tipping the point with metal. Still, it was no more than a heavy stick that dragged along the surface, scraping a V-shaped furrow in the soil. If the soil was light and dry, the clumsy implement did fairly well. But in northern Europe, where damp, heavy clay prevailed, it took backbreaking labor to produce even poor results.

Perhaps out of hardship, the Slavs in northern Europe developed a new plow that would cut deeply into the heavy soil; their invention soon spread throughout Europe. The moldboard plow's key elements were a knife blade that slashed vertically into the ground, the plowshare that sliced horizontally through it to the grassroots level, and back of these two blades, the shaped board that turned the cut slices of soil over to the side.

The more advanced Chinese had long used a superior plow with its moldboard made of metal. But in Europe the peasants' new plow made a powerful difference in farming. Coupling it to a team of oxen, they could now farm formerly virgin land, clear forests, and cultivate wasteland.

Like many inventions, the new plow changed ways of working and living. It was costly to make and maintain, and you needed six to eight oxen to pull it, so its use on small plots of land was pointless. It led peasants to combine their small plots into larger workable fields. Members of these communal groups no longer acted solely on their own individual needs. They had to consider the needs of others in relation to the contribution of each to the joint enterprise—in land, in oxen, in labor.

How the Renaissance emerged from the Middle Ages

For many centuries the subsistence economy of the feudal society of Europe seemed fixed, with few changes noticeable. But by the end of the 12th century there was indirect evidence of change. The population became larger and larger; on the average people were living longer, famines happened less often, and the peasants were better fed and clothed.

With their food production rising, the peasants could go beyond production for the sake of survival to an economy of exchange. Farmers chose to cultivate those plants best suited to their soil and most easily saleable in the nearby towns, such as wine or wool or plants useful as medicines and dyes. On the edge of every town there sprang up market gardens and orchards to satisfy the appetite for those products.

One often ignored aspect of the improved production of food is its influence on the Crusades. Between the 10th and the 14th centuries Christian Europe carried on nine wars to free the Holy Land from the Muslims. During that time not only was there a substantial increase in the food supply, but also considerable improvement in its nutritional value. One result, says the British historian Reay Tannahill, "was a growing population that was better fed and more energetic than ever before—dynamic, ripe for action, ideal tools for the aggressive imperialism of the Crusades."

The cost of a prolonged Crusade—the distance to be traveled from western Europe to Jerusalem was 3,000 miles (4,828 kilometers)—was enormous. Who paid it? The people, of course, all of them: Landlord or peasant, noble or merchant, clergy or layman were all heavily taxed under the threat of excommunication. Many joined not in the interests of Christ but to get rich on plunder.

As agriculture improved in the late Middle Ages, and farmers began marketing their products, it helped to revive village and urban life. Meanwhile, Crusaders returned home with a hunger for the luxuries such as spices, silks, and jewels that they had discovered on their travels. International trade flourished, and by 1400 western society was moving from the Dark Ages into the brilliant era of the Renaissance.

It is hard for us to picture what European life was like for peasants at the dawn of the Renaissance. From Russia in the East to the Atlantic shore in the West the continent was covered by an almost trackless forest. Beneath the canopy of trees lived about 70 million people. The small cities were usually located by the sea, rivers, or trading centers. Large metropolitan centers would not appear until the Industrial Revolution some 300 years later.

About 85 percent of the population were peasants. (By 1500 serfdom had declined in Western Europe.) They lived in tiny villages of under a hundred people, and these hamlets were often 15 miles (24 kilometers) or more apart, sitting in the midst of forest. The more prosperous peasants dwelt in rambling structures of wood, mud, and thatch, with dung heaps piled high just beyond the door. Within the same walls as the family you'd find a pigpen, a henhouse, cattle sheds, corncribs, straw, and hay. Seeping below the floor of clay and rushes would be spittle and vomit, rotted scraps of meat and fish "and other filth unnameable," reported Erasmus, the Dutch humanist, who visited these homes. The smells were stupefying, he said.

Everyone in the peasant family slept in a single room, where soot flaked off the walls and ceiling. The one gigantic bedstead was piled up with straw pallets alive with vermin. Parents, children, and grandparents piled on top of the huge bed, with hens and pigs on the floor around them. If a stranger came by, he was invited to join the others on the family bed.

Peasant menus across the continents were plain and monotonous. In northern Europe it was dark bread, cabbage, beans, or salt pork. In China it was rice, vegetables, and maybe a mouthful of pork; in Mexico, maize pancakes or beans, with tomatoes and peppers. Yet if a good cook ruled the kitchen, a cook who knew how to make use of the farm's seasonal produce, the family would eat better. The upper classes, of course—the nobility, the prosperous merchants, the bishops—ate much better. A variety of dishes—fish, chicken, meats, game—were placed on the table at the same time, and the diners chose whatever they liked to pile up on their platters. After the meal came dessert—sweets and spicy confections.

Table manners were terrible, among all classes. Not until the 1600s did cutlery come into wide use. People ate with their fingers, transferring each morsel separately from the serving dish to the mouth. Gluttons dipped their hands into a dish almost to the elbow. Napkins, like forks, were not used.

Some people, after gnawing a bone, put it back in the serving dish. The proper thing was to drop it on the floor, which was covered with rushes to smother the garbage. If people blew their noses with their fingers, picked a scab, or scratched a body part, that same unwashed hand went into the common dishes. Hovering over the table was the fetid air of filthy clothing and bodies, for washing either was rarely done.

How the desire for spices changed history

It was in the realm of food that one of the great changes in European habits came about. The desire for spices arose in part from the monotony of the diet in the Middle Ages and from the lack of effective means of preserving food, especially meat. The spices, imported by land and sea routes, which traversed tremendous distances under extremely difficult conditions, brought fantastically high prices when the products reached western markets.

By the 15th century spices had become so important to the West that several nations of Europe cast about for ways to gain control of the products and reduce their cost. In the process, Columbus set out to find an ocean passage to the lands of spices in the Far East by sailing west across the Atlantic. Instead, he landed in the Americas. He died still mistakenly believing he had reached the Orient. His first voyage to America in 1492, however, was an unparalleled historic event with far-reaching effects. It reshaped the thinking of people and marked the end of medievalism. And it began a vast colonial enterprise, exploiting people and resources, nearly annihilating the Indians, and enslaving Africans.

When the two cultures—that of the Europeans and that of the Indians—collided, it ended with the Europeans dominant. But the Indians exerted a strong cultural influence on their white conquerors. The Indians supplied the Europeans with foods that were new to them and taught them to plant and hunt with Indian methods. More than 50 new foods first domesticated by Indians were carried back to the Old World, including turkeys, maize, potatoes, pumpkins, squash, peppers, tomatoes, peanuts, vanilla, avocados, chocolate, several kinds of beans, pineapples, red peppers and green peppers, tapioca . . .

The Americas also benefited. Columbus brought vegetable seeds, wheat, chickpeas, and sugarcane to the Caribbean on his later voyages. In time, with the Europeans or Africans, came cows, bananas, rice, citrus fruits, yams, cowpeas, coconuts, breadfruit, and coffee.

How the conquistadors brought chocolate to the world

Shortly before Pizarro discovered the potato in Peru, another Spanish conquistador, Hernán Cortés, discovered chocolate in Mexico. The Aztec king, Montezuma II, welcomed Cortés with a great feast topped off with a serving of chocolate in golden cups.

The drink was not like the chocolate we know today. The roasted ground seeds of the cacao tree were mixed with cold fermented corn mash and wine or water. It was then flavored with vanilla, hot spices, and perhaps a lick of honey. But neither this novel drink nor anything else the Aztecs could offer appeased Cortés's passion for loot. He grabbed huge amounts of gold and destroyed Aztec temples. With his soldiers he conquered the Aztec empire and turned their flourishing civilization into an enslaved Spanish colony.

Upon his return to Spain in 1528, Cortés carried along with the treasures of Mexico cacao beans and the methods of processing the seeds into a chocolate drink.

In Mexico the cacao bean was valued so highly that many native groups used them as a form of money—so many beans for a rabbit, so many to buy a slave. Conquered Indians would pay sacks of cacao beans as tribute to the victors.

In Spain, royalty did its best to keep the production and consumption of chocolate a tightly guarded monopoly. Although many of the new foods found in Latin America could be grown in Europe, the tropical cacao tree could not. The drink was kept a secret by the court for some 80 years after its introduction. Monks were assigned the task of roasting and grinding the precious beans and then shaping the powder into tablets.

In the 1600s an Italian merchant managed to sneak chocolate out of Spain and introduced it to Italy. From there it migrated to Austria, to Holland, to France. At that time it was regarded as a medicine quite as much as a food. By the mid-1600s the English were enjoying it. In London it was fashionable for upper-class Englishmen to stop by chocolate houses for a cup of the delicious brew. In the Caribbean and Latin America almost everyone—colonists and natives alike—drank it. It reached North America more slowly, imported mostly from Europe at terribly high prices. But in the mid-1700s the cacao bean began to come in directly from the Caribbean, and chocolate grew rapidly in popularity and economic importance. Baker's, the oldest food company in the United States, opened in Dorchester, Massachusetts, in 1765. It was the first to make chocolate in the colonies.

Say candy, and almost everyone thinks first of chocolate. Back in 1894, Milton Hershey figured out how to make a bar of chocolate and began to sell Hershey bars. People like chocolate by itself or prepared in foods: pies, puddings, cakes, cookies, ice cream, hot and cold drinks. It's also used to make medicine taste better and to give color to dark breads. In Italy, Spain, and Mexico they sometimes add it to traditional meat dishes. The Swiss don't take it as a special treat. When a housewife goes out to shop and buys bread, milk, and vegetables, she also picks up a quarter pound of chocolate as the day's ration of candy. Like oil, chocolate is a cash cow for the few regions that can grow the cacao bean. Today West Africa is the main producer.

Swiss families more than 100 years ago created a chocolate empire, far from the regions where the cacao beans are grown. In 1875, by adding milk to chocolate, Swiss innovators outpaced the industry in other countries. Soon after, they used cocoa butter to create silky chocolate that melted in the mouth. Though Swiss chocolatiers still lead the world, Switzerland's biggest companies now manufacture largely outside of the country.

More than merely a flavor, however delicious, chocolate is a food with considerable nutritional value. A 3.5-ounce (99-gram) chocolate bar has about 500 calories. That's equal to the amount in 5 ounces (142 grams) of cheese, or 2 pounds (0.9 kilogram) of bananas. It's very high in carbohydrates; that makes it a fast energy food. It is also rich in fat and a good source of B vitamins and minerals too. Like tea and coffee, it contains caffeine, but a cup of cocoa has only half the stimulants found in a cup of coffee.

Despite the happy custom of giving a heart-shaped box of chocolates to your beloved, there is no chemical evidence that chocolate is a sexual stimulant.

How tea went from luxury to necessity

"Not for all the tea in China . . ."

Those words from a popular song made most of us believe that tea originated in that country and has always been identified with it. But the plant really originated somewhere else in Asia—in the Burma-India region. Probably it was introduced into China by Buddhist monks in the eighth century A.D. as a new exotic drink. Compared to rice or Chinese cabbage, tea was a relatively recent addition to the Chinese food menu.

Tea is one of the four great caffeine plants; the others are coffee, cacao, and cola. The tea bush is beautiful, something like the white-flowered camellia. The legend of how tea entered China holds that the monk Bodhidharma, who introduced Zen to China, meditated before a wall and fell asleep. Furious with himself, he cut off his eyelids, which fell to the ground and grew into tea bushes. (Apparently the Buddhists used tea to keep awake during meditation.)

A big factor in creating tea's popularity was a book of the eighth century—*The Classic of Tea*, by Lu Yiü. It launched the ritualized devotion of tea that continues to this day in East Asia. The Japanese tea ceremony expresses it.

The first cargoes of tea arrived in Europe in the early 1600s. The Portuguese, the Dutch, and the English imported it from China. The tea plant was a bush from which the peasants plucked the leaves. These were dried by heat from a fire or in the heat of the sun. The leaves were rolled by hand and sent out in large chests lined with lead into which they were crushed like grapes.

Tea entered England in 1646, brought in by the East India Company. Within 100 years, fleets of tea ships were unloading at almost all ports of Europe and in America as well. Like all new things, it met with opposition. In England drinking tea was denounced as a filthy custom; it was said that men lost their stature and women their beauty by the use of tea. Yet tea drinking spread with startling speed. Samuel Johnson, the literary sage, called himself "a hardened and shameless tea drinker who for twenty years diluted his meals with only the infusion of the fascinating plant; who with tea amused the evening, with tea solaced the midnight, and with tea welcomed the morning."

It was estimated that every person in England and the American colonies drank a pound (0.4 kilogram) of tea a year. The British government seized on a tea tax for fresh revenue, which gave the American colonies another reason for revolt.

China, however, remained the largest producer and consumer of tea. The Chinese became so knowledgeable they could distinguish between teas grown in various localities. They developed a good many varieties, flavoring some with ginger or tangerine peel. Some teas were sold in cake form or powdered.

They prized it too as medicine, holding that it relieved tiredness, repaired the eyesight, strengthened the will, and delighted the soul. Tea was not only taken internally, but was often applied externally in the form of a paste to ease arthritic pain. Lu Wu, a Chinese poet of the eighth century, in a celebrated three-volume work, the *Ch'a Ching*, formulated "The Holy Scripture of Tea." In it he describes the nature of the plant, how to gather and select the leaves, and what equipment and methods to use to make, serve, and drink tea. In northern China, where the tea plant did not grow well, the poorer people knew it only as a luxury they could not afford. Instead, they sipped hot water——giving it the name of tea—with as much pleasure as the upper classes drank the real thing.

In Japan, the tea ceremony, says Kakuzo Okakura, "became a religion of the art of life." The tearoom, introduced in the 16th century, "was an oasis, and the ceremony an improvised drama whose plot was woven about the tea, the flowers, and the paintings."

While just about everybody drank tea in China and Japan, it did not become that popular in the rest of the Far East. Next to the Chinese and the English, the Russians became the world's most devoted tea drinkers, keeping it warm all day in samovars. When they first encountered tea, in the 1700s, they boiled up the leaves with milk and butter.

It took some time for tea drinkers to realize that the quality of the water used makes a big difference in the drink. And they soon learned that the relatively expensive price didn't matter that much, because you could make about 300 cups of tea out of just 1 pound of the stuff. Besides, in those early years people believed tea was good for your health and added years to your life. The merchants, of course, with their usual hoopla, introduced tea as the sure cure for headaches, apoplexy, paralysis, colic, gallstones, and a host of other afflictions.

At first tea was a luxury item in America. Only the rich drank it. Gradually, from the 1750s on, it became an everyday drink. (Remember the Boston Tea Party in 1773? The colonists hated having their favorite drink taxed for the benefit of the king.) By the 1830s, however, coffee, a stronger stimulant with a stronger flavor, was beating out tea in popularity.

How sugar became the world's leading crop

Whoever thinks of the history behind that teaspoon of sugar when you sweeten your cup of tea or coffee? So many people find it hard to do without sugar that sugarcane is now the world's leading crop. The annual tonnage of the plant produced today nearly equals that of the number two and three crops combined—wheat and corn.

As far back as 7000 B.C. the people of New Guinea had domesticated sugarcane, the plant that is one of the two major sources of sugar. (The other is the sugar beet.) Many thousands of years later, when the Europeans were colonizing the New World, Spain began cultivating sugar in Cuba and Hispaniola. As disease and slaughter wiped out much of the local populations, the planters turned to Africa to solve the labor shortage.

The owners of slave ships grew rich on the profits of carrying slaves from the African coast across the Atlantic to the Caribbean region. Eager for a share of the new wealth, the Portuguese combined enslavement in Africa with sugar production in Brazil. This came about with the blessing of Pope Nicholas V, who called for reducing "to perpetual slavery the pagans and other enemies of Christ" in Africa.

Greed knew no racial or ethnic barrier. The captains of the slave ships got complete cooperation from the African monarchs and merchants of the Gold Coast who were ready to exchange people for cloth, hardware, liquor, and firearms.

So the slave trade prospered along with the sugar producers. There were only 5 sugar plantations in Brazil in 1550; by 1623 there were 350. Other European powers soon cut themselves in for a slice of the handsome profits. The Dutch, the English, the French, and the Danes took over several of the Caribbean islands to expand sugar cultivation.

In the 1700s promoters on the payroll of the West Indies sugar planters were touting the value of sugar for whatever ailed you. Sugar, they claimed, was beneficial to everyone, of whatever class or age or sex. A skin problem? Try our hand lotion made from sugar. Bad teeth? Try our powdered sugar. Want to give up tobacco? Try our sugar snuff.

As Dr. Slingsby, a character in Barry Unsworth's novel about the slave trade, *Sacred Hunger*, put it:

> Sir, sugar has a thousand uses, it is the most versatile of all commodities in the world. It is first of all a food, of course, and an excellent one. A man can live on the products of sugar alone for many weeks altogether without the smallest detriment, as I have proved upon my own person. But sugar is also a preservative, a solvent, a stabilizer. . . . It improves the eyesight, preserves the hair and sweetens the blood. Sir, there is no end to the virtues of sugar.

In America, as people took to drinking tea and coffee, sugar went along with them as a sweetener. It was also eaten in the refined "loaf" form and, more cheaply, as molasses. Sugar and sweetened drinks became so popular that they were considered necessities of life even for the poor. Today almost every packaged food contains sugar. It has became "the universal flavoring."

Sugar became so important a product that it reshaped colonial empires. The Dutch traded the city of New Amsterdam (renamed New York) to England in exchange for the sugar lands of Surinam. And France gave over all of Canada to Britain to acquire Guadeloupe. The craving for sugar seemed to have no limit. In the late 1980s, Americans were consuming 126 pounds (57 kilograms) per person and the British 80 pounds (36 kilograms).

Is sugar good for you or not? In 1986 a medical task force of the U.S. Food and Drug Administration reported on a study of sugar's effects. The conclusions: "We can now state categorically that there is no evidence at all to link sugar with obesity, diabetes, high blood pressure, hyperactivity or heart disease."

■ ■ ■

How sugar spread the use of slave labor

Sugar provides an example of how history can hop from island to island, in many parts of the world. Sugarcane was brought from India to Egypt, then to Cyprus in the tenth century, and a hundred years later to Sicily. It was Henry the Navigator of Portugal who sent Sicily's sugarcane to Madeira, the first "sugar island" of the Atlantic. From there, sugar growing moved rapidly to the Azores, the Canaries, the Cape Verde islands and beyond—to the islands of the West Indies.

For the islanders this invasion by a foreign crop was bad news. Sugar was a crop grown for export only, a crop that badly upset the balance of the island's economy. And all this was done not for the benefit of the native islanders themselves but to satisfy the craving of a Europe clamoring for sugar and for the profits to be derived from it. It was the sugar plantations that would spread the use of slave labor.

In the United States, the commercial sugar industry began with President Thomas Jefferson's purchase of Louisiana in 1803. Immigrants to Louisiana from the troubled Caribbean sugar islands experimented with raising and manufacturing cane sugar, using African-American slaves. Work on a sugar plantation was harsher than labor on the cotton or tobacco fields. Only on rice plantations were conditions as bad. Few slaves were able to escape to freedom. They did the backbreaking work of building the American sugar industry, but they got nothing for their efforts.

■ ■ ■

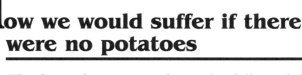How we would suffer if there were no potatoes

The Spanish conquistadors who followed Columbus to the Americas were looking for gold, silver, and precious stones. But they found a richness of food as well—fish, deer, wild llama, bear, puma, fox. Pizarro, invading Peru, saw both the guinea pig and the duck in every household. But the basic Peruvian diet was vegetables, the potato chief among them. Grown by the Inca high in the Andes mountains for thousands of years, the potato, when circulated among the continents, would become one of the four most important crops in the world.

The Inca had learned how to preserve the potato by a process of freezing and drying. They grew it in many sizes, tiny as a nut to big as an apple. Both its shape and coloring varied. (Today in the Andes a peasant can tell the difference between 300 varieties of potato, and he will cook his stew with as many as 20 to 40 varieties, carefully balanced.)

Unimpressed at first by this funny looking new vegetable, the Spaniards soon found out it was the staple food of the mountain people. If so useful to them, why could it not become useful to people anywhere?

The potato's migration began when the Spaniards packed it aboard their ships heading home with the loot stolen from Peru. The vegetable would help feed the sailors on the long voyage. Later Sir Francis Drake, the first Englishman to captain a round-the-world tour, found the potato in Chile. He fed his crew with it and then carried the vegetable to England. By the late 1500s potatoes were being grown in Italy and then in Germany, Austria, Switzerland, and finally in France. Eventually potato crops took hold all around the world, becoming in many countries—like Ireland—the staple food. It is about the most perfect source of nutrition so far discovered. The health of the people of at least 130 countries would suffer if suddenly they had to do without the potato. Worldwide, the value of the lowly vegetable is estimated at about $100 billion a year.

How wheat became the world's largest cereal crop

Wheat is believed to have been growing since the time of the Old Stone Age and cultivated for at least 6,000 years. It is the world's largest cereal-grass crop, second as a staple only to rice. Bakers like it because, unlike other cereals, wheat has a high amount of gluten, a protein that provides the elasticity needed for making good bread.

Wheat's grain is very nutritious. On average it consists of 70 percent carbohydrate, 12 percent protein, 2 percent fat, and 1.8 percent minerals. It only requires intensive labor at the spring sowing and the autumn harvest. By contrast, rice growers have to tend the paddy fields throughout the year. But wheat farmers have the time and freedom to do more. They can grow secondary crops, reclaim land, build, fight, and do politics.

The trouble with wheat is it quickly wears out the soil. In ancient times land could only retain its fertility if the wheat fields were regularly left fallow and manured by domestic animals. That, by necessity, led to the traditional pattern of mixed arable and livestock farming, allowing a varied diet of cereals, vegetables, and meat.

There are over 30,000 varieties of wheat, but the three major types are hard wheat, soft wheat, and durum wheat. This last is used often in semolina, the basis for quality pasta. In the United States, wheat is also identified by the time of year it is sown—in the spring or in the fall.

Wheat has been cultivated since ancient times in Egypt. The grain from the Nile valley fed many in the days of the Roman Empire. Later, wheat did the same for Byzantium, for the Arabs at Damascus, and for the Ottoman Empire. At the time of the Spanish colonization of the Americas, wheat was brought from the Old World to the New World. Portuguese traders brought wheat to parts of Africa, to the offshore Atlantic islands, and to northern Europe.

The market for wheat was reshaped in the latter part of the 19th century when production under capitalism took a great leap forward. It intensified the demand for raw materials and foodstuffs, creating a vastly expanded market of worldwide scope. As some regions began to specialize in the production of this or that raw material or food crop, it meant that other areas had to raise crops to feed those producers. England offers one example. It had fed itself and even exported agricultural surplus in the 18th century. But at the close of the 19th century it became dependent on foreign suppliers for four-fifths of its wheat and two-fifths of its meat. That kind of reliance on outside sources happened too in the cotton belt of the American South. It came to rely entirely on western wheat.

In the American Midwest and West, before the Civil War, cultivators of wheat advanced into the Great Plains with the deep plow and the mechanical reaper. After the war, railroad construction and the advent of the tramp steamer made overseas export of wheat increasingly profitable. The transcontinental railroad helped carry farmers and tools west to the new lands. It led to the creation of great wheat farms worked with migratory labor. But by the 1880s, as better farm machinery was developed, the farms operated by migrant labor were replaced with farms operated by households. When the combined harvester-thresher appeared in the 1880s, it became possible for a two-man household, such as father and son, to carry on successful wheat production on 200-acre (81-hectare) farms. They were no longer subsistence farmers, but producers of commodities who bought their machinery on the market and sold their product into a market in return. Vast expanses of the continent had become a granary.

The Americans were able to sell their wheat in Europe at lower prices than the European farmers. The flood of cheap American grain into Europe caused a crisis in European peasant agriculture. The result was to drive millions of ruined peasants to seek new livelihoods in prospering America.

Around the same time, Argentina and Canada also became great wheat producers, selling huge amounts abroad. The wheat of southern Russia too entered the world market; 90 percent of its crop was exported through the port of Odessa to western Europe. The Russian system of serfdom on the landed estates was gradually replaced by wage labor, working increasingly with machinery.

■ ■ ■

How rice feeds half the globe

Rice is the most useful plant known to the world. It is the basic and sometimes only food of almost half the world's population.

Among China's food crops, rice by modern times had become the great staple. But not the only one. Today rice provides about 40 percent of China's standard foods, partly because of a recent shift toward wheat, potatoes, and maize. Still, rice remains the primary grain for half to two-thirds of China's people.

The people of the Yangtze delta appear to have been the first to cultivate rice, sometime around 5000 B.C.. But rice may have been domesticated independently in several places, especially because it lends itself to different methods of cultivation. As China's population increased, so did China's growing dependence on agriculture and the expansion and improvement of it. Eventually the gap between the rich and powerful and the poor and weak members of society widened. Peasants had no surplus to save; they could only invest in children. They wanted more hands to work the land and to support them in old age.

By the 12th century China knew many varieties of rice—pink, yellow, white, mature rice, and winter rice, each with its characteristic flavor or fragrance. Some people ate a huge amount of it daily, as much as 2 pounds, five ounces (1 kilogram), not always in the form of grain, but in flour, in wine, and in many different snacks.

Besides China, rice is a staple for parts of India, Indonesia, Japan, and Southeast Asia. Rice entered the Americas with West-African slaves who carried it into Barbados, the West Indies island, in the early 1700s. They brought technical knowledge of where and how to plant it because of their experience with rice in their homelands. Rice cultivation then moved north to Georgia, the Carolinas, and nearby districts. Today the major rice-growing states are Arkansas, Missouri, Mississippi, Texas, Louisiana, and California.

It took expert knowledge of agricultural techniques and equipment to make rice production a success. Most of it in the pre-Civil War South was drudgery of the worst kind, under the worst conditions. And done by slaves. Rice took the heaviest concentration of slaves—more than for tobacco or cotton—anywhere in the South. Many of the rice plantations had from 300 to 1,000 slaves. Few of them lived long, for although rice production was a highly profitable business, it was rife with brutality that meant an appalling death rate for the slaves.

Today scientists are working to develop a "super rice" to feed Asia, where 90 percent of the rice crop is grown and consumed. It is an urgent task because Asia's population is expanding while its farmland shrinks. The rice plant needs an overhaul because its stems are weak and slender, many of its stalks are unproductive, and it is vulnerable to insects and disease.

That is why the International Rice Research Institute is trying to redesign the delicate green plant into a more effective grain producer. A great step forward was made in the late 1960s when the researchers came up with "miracle rice," which nearly doubled the world's rice harvest. Through experiments in plant breeding, scientists around the world developed 500 varieties of miracle rice. Some of these are now used by about half the rice farmers in the tropics.

But as world population continues to grow, the spread of industry and of big cities has cut down on the land and water available to farmers. And as rural people move into cities, the farm labor supply drops too.

Every day now 2.5 billion people eat rice. That number will jump to 4 billion by the year 2025. Science and the farmer will have to produce 70 percent more rice from less land and less water and less labor—if millions are not to starve.

How wars have brought on starvation

While raising food has been one of humankind's chief activities for countless thousands of years, so has making war. The two are closely intertwined. As the population grew in the earliest human societies, the local food supply diminished. People were forced to migrate in search of food. Group competed with group for subsistence. Early warfare probably developed because of the struggle over adequate food.

But whether or not the drive for food was the cause of a particular war, warfare itself has always meant hunger or starvation for many. Take the Hundred Years War: Fought between England and France in a quarrel over which country controlled what land, it broke out in 1337 and did not end until 1453.

The farmlands were devastated, and the population savagely reduced by fighting, by famine, and by the Black Plague. The men who fought as soldiers risked death or mutilation on the battlefield. At home, women, the very young, and the elderly, deprived of sufficient food, died of malnutrition or of disease against which their weakened bodies could offer little resistance.

One of the most ancient weapons in warfare was to lay siege to a stronghold of the enemy and, by preventing any aid from coming in, starve the occupants into surrender. The Hebrew Bible tells of the siege of Jericho. And the Greek poet Homer in his epic, the *Iliad*, describes the siege of Troy. The chronicles of the Middle Ages are chock full of accounts of sieges laid to the enemies' castles. In the American Civil War, the Confederate city of Petersburg in Virginia was besieged for nine months by the troops of Union General Ulysses S. Grant.

In modern times the longest siege of a city was that of Leningrad (now St. Petersburg) by the armies of the Nazi dictator Adolf Hitler. His tank forces had invaded the Soviet Union in June of 1941, and by December they had reached the gates of Leningrad. For over two years the Germans kept more than 2 million men, women, and children penned up in the city, soon to starve by the tens of thousands as they consumed their supply of food and all help was cut off. They were deprived of light, heat, and bread, and the only water to drink was dipped out of the city's filthy canals. Cats, dogs, pigeons, every pet disappeared into the mouths of the starving. Parents tried to keep children off the streets for fear they would be kidnapped and eaten. Fresh corpses were dug out of cemeteries and butchered for food. "Meat patties" were sold on the street, made of ground-up human flesh.

Not until January 27, 1944—after 900 days—did Russian army groups succeed in liberating Leningrad. By that time three-fourths of the people had died of starvation or disease.

How mass hunger kills millions

For lack of food, people starve to death.

The tragedy of mass hunger—they call it famine—has taken untold millions of lives throughout history. Despite the immense increase in the productivity of agriculture, many still starve, as they did long ago. The book of Genesis, in the Hebrew Bible, tells of the seven fat years in ancient Egypt, followed by the seven lean years when "famine was over all the face of the earth." But Joseph saved the people of Egypt from starvation because, interpreting Pharaoh's dream of lean years to come, he had stored up food enough to feed all.

History contains many references to the outbreak of famine in all parts of the world. Toward the end of the first century A.D., a people called the Huns rode out of Mongolia and crossed the steppes into southeast Europe. Their exodus was forced by famine in the lands north of China. In A.D. 125 an invasion of locusts devastated large areas of Italy's crops, which brought on a famine and its common companion, the plague. Hundreds of thousands died.

In the ninth and tenth centuries the Viking longships came down from Scandinavia to devastate lands great distances from their base. They roved far and wide in search of loot and slaves, reducing communities and churches and monasteries to smoking ruins, razing their crops, and carrying off their livestock. Behind them they left starving victims.

In the tenth century alone, Europe endured 20 famines, some of them lasting three or four years. Hunger became so intense that people began to devour each other. Bands of murderers trapped travelers on the roads, killed them, cooked their flesh, and sold it to the highest bidders.

In China in the 12th century a famine in the northern provinces led people to cannibalism. There they called what they were eating "pork" or "mutton." During the Middle Ages cannibalism, born of hunger, was recorded in Bohemia, Silesia, and Poland.

When bad harvests occurred, rich landowners and the peasants who had small farms held what food there was for their own use. The townfolk, who had no land, suffered for lack of food. When the shortage brought on famine, and the towns threatened violence to get food, the lords tried to forestall revolt by forcing the peasants to give up what they had stored.

Famine in many parts of Europe was a common experience. For the poor, the food problem was never quite solved. A great famine seized parts of Europe from 1315 to 1317. Even the most fertile provinces did not escape it. Ypres, for example, a rich French town near the coast, failed to store enough food to prevent some 3,000 people—one-fifth of the population—from dying of starvation within six months.

The historian Fernand Braudel estimated that France had an average of 11 general famines per century from the 10th to the 19th century. The story of just one city—Florence, Italy—suggests how bad things could get. Florence suffered serious hunger in 111 of the 400 years between 1371 and 1791, and people sometimes resorted to cannibalism to survive.

Or take Russia—between A.D. 971 and the 19th century it went through 125 famine years. One of the worst famines struck rural Russia in 1890. The peasants of the Volga region faced starvation during that long, dry summer. Wells and ponds dried up, the scorched earth cracked, cattle died by the roadsides. The harvest yield was but a tiny fraction of the normal. The area threatened by famine spread to 17 provinces, from the Ural mountains to the Black Sea, an area double the size of France, with a population of 36 million. As the hungry peasants weakened, cholera and typhus struck, killing half a million people by the end of 1892.

The Czar's government was too slow and clumsy to cope with the crisis. It showed itself to be careless and callous when it allowed grain merchants to ship food abroad that could have been used to feed the starving peasants.

The government refused to admit the existence of a famine, calling it only "a poor harvest." The czar allowed hundreds of thousands to die of starvation rather than to invite help from outside. For to do that would have been admitting his own government's failure. The newspapers were forbidden to print reports of the famine, though some managed to hint at it. It only convinced people that there was a government conspiracy to hide the truth. Leo Tolstoy, the great writer, braved the emperor's anger by publicizing in every way open to him the extent and horror of the calamity.

With no aid offered, riots broke out, which troops were sent in to put down. Finally, unable to handle the crisis, the government called on the public to form committees to provide famine relief. The response was tremendous. People of all kinds and in great numbers volunteered their time, their labor, their skills, their money, and in some cases, their lives. Hundreds of committees formed to help raise money for the famine victims. Students volunteered for relief work by going out into the rural districts to help on the spot. Tolstoy, always a partisan of the weak and oppressed, gave up his writing to pitch into the relief campaign. With his two eldest daughters he organized hundreds of canteens in the famine region while his wife raised money from abroad. Anton Chekhov, who was a doctor as well as a playwright, treated cholera victims in the villages and factories and monasteries.

The social conscience of the public was awakened by the famine crisis, while the czarist bureaucratic system was discredited. Public debate on the causes of the famine and on the need for social and political reforms continued to rage for many years. One young woman, Lydia Dan, said that the famine had shown the youth of her generation that "the Russian system was completely bankrupt. It felt as though Russia was on the brink of something."

It was. For in 1917 a revolutionary upheaval began that soon climaxed in the seizure of power by the Communists. Four years later, in 1921, Russia suffered another famine, with five million people, mainly peasants, dying.

Worse was to come within ten years. The trouble began in 1929 when the government deported millions of so-called "kulaks," or the slightly better-off peasants, to the Arctic, where they endured great suffering and death. The Communists set about collectivizing the farms, in effect abolishing private property in land, and placing the farmers under Communist control.

This was part of a policy to crush elements seen as hopelessly hostile to the Communist regime—the peasantry and the nationalists of the Ukraine region, where so many of them lived. It was done by what historians call the "terror-famine." Stalin's officials set quotas for grain delivery far above the possible level, thus taking away all the grain and fodder. By 1933 a terrible famine had set in. Whole families died, houses fell apart, village streets grew empty as the Communists prevented help from outside from reaching the starving.

The Ukraine, a great stretch of territory with some 40 million inhabitants, lost a quarter of its people.

How the potato blight devastated Ireland

Everywhere people connect Ireland with the potato, as they connect rice with China. The potato reached Ireland in the 16th century, just as the soldiers of Queen Elizabeth I crushed Irish revolts against British rule. The potato met the desperate need of the poverty-stricken peasants, for it was easy to prepare and could feed both the family and the livestock. It was what kept the Irish alive in a terrible time.

By 1800, for nine-tenths of the Irish, the potato had largely replaced the old diet of meat, milk, and oatmeal. It enabled subsistence on a tiny holding, providing food for nine months of the year. Though people did not know it then, the potato is the most natural source of nutrition so far discovered. The Irish depended more and more on it as the harsh British rule stifled their ability to make a living. The majority of Ireland's people held little or no land of their own. They usually paid rent in the form of labor for the benefit of their absentee landlords.

As Ireland's population kept increasing so did mass poverty. The sufferings of the Irish, said a British Commission report in 1845, were "greater than the people of any other country in Europe had to sustain."

Then, as the summer of 1845 began, a blight struck the potato fields. The disease spread quickly, laying whole fields waste in a few hours, sweeping over the land, even invading barns and houses to ruin stored potatoes.

The killer was a new fungus, *Phytophthora infestans*, a microscopic organism that had hit first North America and then reached Europe, probably in a diseased tuber carried on a ship. Within six months after the crop's failure, famine set in. The blight redoubled in 1846, preventing a new crop from being sown. In 1847 the disease let up, but it returned, full force, in 1848 and 1849.

In many districts people starved by the hundreds, eating anything, even rotted potatoes they knew had killed pigs and cattle. As the blight hung on year after year, bands of Irish wandered the roads, begging for food, looking "more like famished wolves than men," said one observer. Cabins were deserted, often with unburied corpses inside. Typhus raged through weakened bodies.

Yet, said Gerald Keegan, a schoolteacher at that time, "There is corn and wheat and meat and dairy products in abundance. For putting his hands on any of this, the tenant is liable to prison, even to execution or to exile." All that food was seized by landowners and merchants and shipped for sale to England. Private charities, chiefly the Quakers, tried to help the starving, but they could not cope with so huge a problem. Humane officials who wanted to help relieve the suffering met violent opposition by people who believed government must never interfere with private enterprise. They opposed public aid to the poor, no matter how desperately it was needed.

The Irish famine caused boatloads of starving emigrants to flee to America. Emigration was promoted by landlords who wished to rid their large estates of the helpless, starving, disease-ridden tenants. Tens of thousands died at sea or soon after landing in America.

Ireland's population loss was enormous in the years between 1845 and 1851. It has been computed at 2.25 million—through starvation, disease, and emigration. This, out of a population of 8 million.

 How China's "Great Leap Forward" created famine

The worse famine in history occurred in modern times. It happened in Communist China when 30 million people died of starvation between 1959 and 1961. The sheer numbers seem unbelievable. It's as if the entire population of California had been wiped out.

Any famine is appalling, but this one was worse because it did not occur for "natural" causes—prolonged drought, extraordinary flooding, or blight. No, it was man-made. Nature had nothing to do with it.

In 1949 the Red Army took over China, and the Communist leadership proclaimed the People's Republic. Industry and agriculture were soon forcibly collectivized. In 1958, Mao Zedong, the Communist leader, unleashed "The Great Leap Forward" campaign. He wanted to bring China to world leadership through a vast effort of mobilization. It meant building millions of backyard furnaces to smelt scrap metal into "steel." It meant replacing the time-honored methods of Chinese farmers—whose yields were as high as possible without the benefits of technology—with pseudoscientific methods of agriculture borrowed from the Soviet Union where they had already shown they did not work.

The results were catastrophic. Backyard furnaces turned the peasants' tools and cookware into useless molten globs. Millions of farmers were diverted from the land to work on huge construction projects. As farm productivity collapsed, officials too scared to tell the truth reported nonexistent record yields on which huge taxes were then levied, leaving the peasants without enough to live on.

In every part of the vast country in 1959 starvation set in. The weak and elderly were the first to die. But Mao refused to believe reports of food shortages and concluded that the peasants were lying and that greedy farmers were conspiring to hide grain in order to squeeze more supplies from the state. Government agents used brutal torture in the vain attempt to uncover nonexistent hoards of secret food.

People ate cats, dogs, insects. Parents abandoned their starving children on the roadside in the hope that passersby would see them and take pity on them. The Chinese people were forced to the most sickening form of desperation—cannibalism. Human flesh was sold on the market, parents swapped children so people could use them for food without committing the additional sin of eating their own.

Those terrible years are still nearly blank pages in China's history. The Communists managed to hide the very fact of a famine for almost a generation. The truth about the real causes of one of the worst atrocities of all time would have made their practices abominable in the eyes of the whole world.

At last, in early 1962, necessity forced the Chinese leadership to recognize the terrible calamity they had caused. Policy was changed and the artificially made famine came to an end.

How the poor eat

What the poor ate, always and everywhere—except perhaps for the early stage of hunting and gathering—differed markedly from what the rich ate. Take England in the 19th century. Poor people lived on bread. It was the basic building block of the worker's diet. If he was lucky, onions or potatoes or bacon might be added to his bread. But his wife and children often had only bread. For the male who worked and supported the family needed to keep his strength up. Because they were cheaper, he ate cheese rather than butter, and fish rather than meat.

Farm laborers usually had only one hot meal a week. The cooking was done over an open fire, as few of the poor had ovens. A limited diet was bad enough, but even if there was some food to eat, keeping it fresh was a problem. If the poor were lucky enough to have a pig to kill in the autumn, the sides had to be hung up in the chimney to be smoked and preserved. Because there was no refrigeration, the women were always bottling things and making preserves.

Few drank water, because it was impure and unsafe. Beer and ale were downed instead, and later on, tea and coffee. Children enjoyed no better a diet. They might get bread, potatoes and mutton, rice pudding or oatmeal. Fresh milk for the town poor was too expensive and, besides, was often contaminated before pasteurization was adopted in the 1890s. Few understood then that the young need great amounts of food, and kids often went hungry.

How the rich live

Land, out of which most of our food comes, is a great source of wealth—for those few who own it, of course, not for the many who work it. Let's look at 19th-century England to grasp what being land-rich meant in those days.

At the top of the social ladder were the landed aristocracy. These were old, powerful families with large estates and inherited titles. Their families had lived on their estates for many generations. About a fifth of England was owned by the lords of the land. On the average their estates encompassed 10,000 acres (4,047 hectares). But some had much more, like the Duke of Ancaster who controlled 163,000 acres (65,963 hectares).

To own such vast estates gave a family great prestige. But even more—it brought in rent from the tenant farmers. That was the major source of income for most of the landed gentry and nobility in the 1800s. Good land was not easy to obtain. Much of it was tied up in complex family estates. When the head of the family died, the land passed down the male line, while the women got government securities.

There was more than rental income to be derived from land ownership. It brought political power, social influence, the fun of shooting and hunting and fishing on your own acres, and the pleasure of bossing your tenants around.

Portions of the land and the cottages on them were rented out to farmers who worked the acres by themselves or with rural laborers, supervised by the estate manager. The lords usually spent about five months of the year—August through December—on their estates, and the rest of the time in London or abroad. So they had little to do with the daily management of the estate. Their attention fixed on London, on the court and Parliament and national affairs.

Below the aristocracy came the gentry. These people had much less land, maybe 1,000 to 3,000 acres (405 to 1,214 hectares). They too often rented out the land to tenant farmers.

Next in rank were the yeomen, or gentlemen farmers. Often these small landholders dirtied their own hands working the land themselves. Some, however, were prosperous enough to climb up into the social circle of the gentry. Under the heavy pressure of economic change, however, yeomen often lost their land and became tenant farmers or laborers on the large estates.

At the bottom of the rural world were the farm laborers. They lived in small one- or two-room thatched or slate cottages on an estate or in the local village. Their cottages were usually owned by the local aristocrat. Before 1800 a cottager's family tended to stay on the land for generations, secure in the long leases given them, which were routinely renewed. That changed when the trend to large-scale commercial farming set in. With little compassion, the large landowners ousted the tenants from their cottages as their leases expired.

Short-term or temporary agricultural laborers took over the work, much to the profit of the landlord. He no longer had to care for his labor, in good times or bad. He could hire and fire them at will, unconcerned with what might happen to the poor and landless who did all the work.

How American farm families used to live

In the 19th century the great majority of Americans were farmers—four out of five in 1800, and although commerce and manufacturing expanded, it was still three out of four in 1840. Both men and women shared the work, with the women's responsibility being the farmyard, garden, kitchen, and hearth. Women took care of the poultry, the men took care of the horses, sheep, and cattle.

A woman's round of chores was never done—cooking, cleaning, washing, sewing, mending, and, of course, the rearing of the children. Men's work was more seasonal and more varied from day to day. It was a patriarchal family: The man governed, his work and his decisions were paramount.

The basic rhythm of the farm was plowing, planting, cultivation, and harvest. Corn—which almost every family throughout the country grew—was the staple food in the diets of both people and livestock.

Cooking was at the center of daily work for housewives. Women learned from mothers and grandmothers a way of preparing food that had changed little for the past hundred years. They mastered the skills of salting, pickling, and smoking meat to preserve it. They made wheat or rye bread, johnnycake, or hominy. They stewed, roasted, and fried. Salt, sugar, spices, and coffee came in bulk form and had to be ground or pounded. There was water to be hauled—often long distances—butter and cheese to be made, chickens to be killed, eggs to be gathered, vegetables to be harvested from the garden or root cellar.

Women cooked over a fireplace, using heavy iron pots and kettles that sat on coals or hung on a crane over the fire. The stooping and lifting was very hard on the back. But in the late 1830s the cookstove came into use in the commercial villages and towns where people could afford it. The heating surface on the stove top was waist high, and the lighter-weight pots and kettles made the labor of cooking easier. This stove was the first major cooking appliance, a giant step up from the ancient fireplace and hearth. It was made possible when the technology of cast iron was improved.

If a woman was rich, living on a plantation or in the city, she had servants—or slaves—to do all the chores of cooking and serving and cleaning up. Her task was to plan and supervise their work.

The children in farm families helped with many of the chores, up to their capacity. In 1800 most white children went to school from the ages of 5 to 15. But it was only for a few weeks a year, or maybe two months. Some never entered school and remained illiterate. The children of slaves were denied the right to education. In the South it was a crime to teach a slave to read.

How dirty and smelly can the world get?

Food has other, less pleasant aspects than its nutrition and flavor. What happens to waste? In the early decades of the new American republic, people lived in a dirty and stinking world. The farmyards were slimy with animal wastes. Boots and pants were spattered with manure. On a warm or windy day you could easily tell where the privies were.

The cities were often far worse than the farmyards. Besides trying to sidestep the horse manure that blanketed the streets, walkers had to be wary of household slops—garbage and dirty dishwater tossed blithely out of windows or doors. In some cities pigs by the hundreds or even thousands roamed the streets, eating the garbage. And the pigs themselves befouled the streets. The areas around the wharves and public markets stank with the decaying leftovers of fish, meat, and vegetables.

How much meat do people eat?

How much meat do people eat? And where does it come from?

Scientists studying the eating habits of groups of hunter-gatherers in today's world report they eat about a quarter to a half pound (0.1 to 0.2 kilograms) per person per day. It could be less for those who live in the tropics, rather than the temperate, subarctic, or arctic regions. But their forebears almost certainly ate more meat.

Looking far back into prehistory, around 10,000 B.C., it's speculated that hunters would have brought home enough game to provide at least 2 pounds (1 kilogram) of boneless meat per adult per day. To kill the large animals—mammoth, musk-ox, or bison—needed to feed the group demanded great hunting skills and strength. Hurling a flint-tipped spear through an animal's eye into its brain, flinging a heavy stone to the vital spot on a skull, or crippling a beast by slicing through the heel tendons, required the swiftest reflexes and the keenest coordination of hand and eye.

A mammoth's carcass, after boning at the site of the kill, supplied more than a ton of meat, enough to feed a group of 40 people for a month. What meat people ate depended on what the region offered. In one part of China it was barbecued elephant's trunk, and in another it was mutton, beef, and buffalo. During Marco Polo's stay in China he saw that people ate liver raw, chopped up in garlic sauce. The gentry too ate meat raw.

In the Middle Ages, butchers sold meat in town markets. To guard against robbers stealing food from the stalls, or against merchants who cheated their customers, strict regulations were applied. Butchers now had to sell meat by weight, instead of, as they used to, by the piece. Before this, corrupt butchers would pad out a piece of meat by blowing air between the membranes, making it look bigger. Or since people disliked the taste of lean meat, they'd strip layers of fat off stout oxen and sew them on to lean cuts.

It was a messy trade in other ways. If you were unlucky enough to live near a London slaughterhouse, you saw butchers killing their beasts right out in public streets. They'd tote the entrails and the offal through the town, blood dripping all the way, and toss the filthy stuff into the river, befouling the water.

Much later, in the 1850s, with the advent of rapid transportation by rail, the killing was done some 500 miles (805 kilometers) away, with ready-dressed carcasses shipped to London. Mountains of beef, mutton, pork, and veal arrived the night after it was slaughtered.

The plain people of Europe in the Middle Ages ate mostly bread, water, or ale, and whatever hot broth was in the cauldron, leftover scraps of meat that made a soup thick with the shreds of past meals. The less poor could afford bacon or meat.

How much meat was eaten it's hard to be sure of. Few statistics were kept in medieval times. But in the Italian city of Florence someone recorded that each year "4,000 oxen and calves, 60,000 mutton and sheep, 20,000 she-goats and he-goats, and 30,000 pigs" were consumed. That's about one and a half food animals per person, which suggests appetites were satisfied. Another clue: The household of Charles VI of France ate 200 sheep every week.

It took a long time to figure out ways to preserve meat. In the 1650s cooked meats were preserved for a limited time by covering them with a thick layer of fat, which shut out air. In 1810, when Napoleon was looking for better ways to get food to troops at the front, Nicholas Appert showed how to preserve meat by enclosing it in glass bottles that were corked and heated. The next step was moving from fragile glass containers to unbreakable tin cans. In 1811, Brian Donkin, an Englishman, bought Peter Durand's patent on his invention of the tin can, and soon a canning factory was turning out cured beef, boiled beef, mutton, and veal.

It was more costly to stock up on canned foods, so for some time the customers were chiefly travelers and explorers or passenger ships. Until the middle of the 19th century Australian canned beef and mutton dominated the market. But after the Civil War, American meat-canning factories, which had sprung up in 1817, took the lead in export sales.

A worldwide boom in livestock farming began as the international market for foods expanded. The great American frontier became a huge cattle-breeding ground—with sad effects on people everywhere.

How beef pioneered the assembly line

The average American consumes the meat of seven 1,100-pound (499-kilogram) steers in a lifetime.

What has that love affair with beef cost us—for one thing, water, that precious and scarce resource. It takes about 1,200 gallons (4,542 liters) of water to produce a single boneless beefsteak. Another cost: grain. Livestock now consume nearly one-third of the world's grain harvest, while nearly a billion people go to bed malnourished. A third cost: health. The cholesterol-raising properties of beef can lead to heart disease and strokes. A fourth cost: environmental ruin. The extension of cattle ranges worldwide has led to the burning of rain forests and the desertification of fertile plains. Millions of people in various parts of the world have been displaced from their homelands to make room for cattle grazing.

Cattle were first domesticated in ancient Mesopotamia—not for food, but primarily as sacrificial animals in religious ceremonies. Cattle and horses were brought to the New World by Columbus on his second voyage in 1494. The Spanish longhorn cattle were allowed to run wild, and in a short time they began to outnumber the human population in the West Indies. The animals prospered and eventually spread throughout the Americas.

When vast numbers of settlers moved into the American West, cattle ranching was transformed. The Great Plains were ruthlessly wiped clean of bison, thus depleting the Indians who had depended on the animals. Range cattle took over the land. Financed by American and foreign investors drawn by the prospect of high profit, big-time ranchers entered the business.

A powerful Euro-American cattle industry colonized vast tracts of the American plains. They enjoyed the use of millions of acres of public lands. In effect, they were subsidized by the American taxpayer. Control over the grazing lands was extended to control over the processing and distribution of the food. Meat-processing facilities were created in Chicago, St. Louis, Cincinnati, and Kansas City. In 1850 that industry was valued at $12 million. By 1920 it had climbed to over $4 billion, and the industry was the nation's second-largest employer.

Most people think of the steel or automobile industries as the pioneers in the successful use of mass-production techniques. But it was the meat packers who took the lead. Their stress on speed and efficiency in the manufacturing of meat and in the division of labor became the pattern for 20th-century industry to follow.

The packinghouses were the first to create an assembly line, with the slaughtered animals moving along a conveyer belt. The animals were killed, dismembered, cleaned, and dressed as they passed from worker to worker, each of whom performed some particular step in the process.

The new methods of production created terrible conditions for the workers. The automated conveyer system forced them to work with furious intensity at the pace set by the machinery. The work was both hazardous and hellish. When the packinghouse laborers organized to demand better working conditions and decent pay, the companies resisted with all their power. Some of the bloodiest labor struggles in American history resulted. Not until the late 1930s did the major beef companies negotiate agreements with the unions.

How much has changed in the meat packing industry in the nearly 100 years since Upton Sinclair wrote his exposé of the working conditions in the slaughterhouses? Not much, according to Jeremy Rifkin, author of *Beyond Beef: The Rise and Fall of the Cattle Culture*. "Working conditions," he says, "are still hazardous and unsanitary. Workers are still mercilessly exploited by management. The companies continue to foster inhumane practices on the kill floor and in the chill rooms. The conditions are often primitive, even ghoulish. It's no wonder that employee turnover is as much as 43 percent a month in some plants. Turnover is fueled by the high rate of personal injury, the second highest of any occupation in America."

By speeding up production and cutting costs to increase profits, the beef industry not only treats animals and workers inhumanely, it also increases health risks to the consumers of meat products.

Despite federal laws presumably meant to protect the health of consumers, inspection procedures are still lax or almost absent altogether. The U.S. Department of Agriculture in recent years has given up methods used for decades to ensure minimum health and safety standards. The new system relies on the companies to do spot inspections on a random basis, so dirty and diseased carcasses squeeze by the review process. And the chance of suffering food poisoning after eating beef is all the more likely.

Cattle are everywhere, grazing on all six continents. One out of every 4 acres (1.6 hectares) in the world is pastureland for cattle and other livestock. Every week 90 percent of all American families buy beef. They consume nearly one-fourth of all the beef produced in the world. There are big differences between what well-to-do people eat, and what the poor eat, but on average, Americans consume 65 pounds (29 kilograms) of beef per year.

Gorging on beef does more than harm the health of the consumer. It has brought about a fundamental shift in world agriculture—from food grain to feed grain. The overpopulation of cattle robs the poor of sustenance to feed the rich a steady diet of grain-fed meat. Take the United States. Over 70 percent of American grain produced is fed to livestock. A steer ready for slaughter weighing 1,050 pounds (476 kilograms) has eaten 2,700 pounds (1,225 kilograms) of grain—a huge disproportion. Take just one year's data, compiled by the food economist Frances Moore Lappé: 145 million tons of grain and soybeans were fed to livestock—cattle, poultry, and hogs. Of that feed only 21 million tons were available to human beings after the energy conversion, in the form of meat, poultry, and eggs. The rest, about 124 million tons of grain and soybeans, were unavailable for humans to eat. If the 124 million tons of wasted grain and soy were supplied for human use, says Lappé, it would have fed "the equivalent of one cup of grain for every single human being on Earth every day for a year."

How a muckraker exposed the Beef Trust

In the late 1800s investigative journalists began to publish articles and books exposing what was glaringly wrong with American business and politics. It upset President Theodore Roosevelt, who charged them with being "lurid sensationalists" and contemptuously called them "muckrakers."

That became an honorable term worn proudly by the writers. One of them was the young Upton Sinclair. He spent two years investigating conditions in the Chicago meat industry and wrote a novel called *The Jungle,* a powerful exposé of working conditions in the Chicago slaughterhouses. He wove in the revolting details of how meat was contaminated, how spoiled hams were treated with formaldehyde, how workers fell into vats and meat grinding machines and ended up in sausages that went to consumers' tables. His best-seller roused a national outcry for better regulations of the meatpacking industry.

Public pressure led Roosevelt to order an inquiry into the industry's conditions. As a result, a new tougher federal meat inspection law was passed in 1906. The Big Five meat packers, called "the Beef Trust," saw how they could cleverly turn regulation to their advantage. They lobbied for the bill, and managed to have the government foot the costs for the elaborate system of inspection. They promptly used the new law to advertise that the U.S. inspection stamp on every pound and package of their product guaranteed purity, wholesomeness, and honest labeling.

How many hamburgers can you eat?

At every tick of the watch, 200 Americans buy one or more hamburgers at a fast-food outlet. Americans eat about 27 pounds (12 kilograms) of ground beef per year. Of all the beef consumed, about 40 percent is now ground beef, mostly hamburgers.

McDonald's didn't originate the burger. Chopped beef goes back to the steppes of Eurasia. The medieval Tartars liked raw beef. They seasoned it with salt, pepper, and onion juice. German travelers brought that "steak tartar" home to Hamburg, where cooks shaped it into patties and broiled it. Much later, in the 1800s, German immigrants introduced the "hamburger" to America.

When America became a mobile society in the 1900s, it gave the burger a big boost. The automobile put tens of millions on wheels. The fast-paced life reshaped eating habits. Restaurants in the 1920s began offering burgers to people on the move. But after World War II, the desire for burgers became a craze. By the late 1950s the world was identifying America as much with burgers as with apple pie. As people began moving out of the cities into the sprawling suburbs, they took to barbecuing burgers in their backyard.

By the 1990s, McDonald's, pacesetter of the fast-food industry, had 11,000 restaurants in 52 countries, employing 600,000 people. At home in America, half the population lived within a 3-minute drive to a McDonald's. The chain applies engineering standards for efficiency, speed, and economy to the preparation of burgers, just as the meat packers had done much earlier in their trade. So too do all the other fast-food outlets that are found everywhere now.

How the pizza came to America

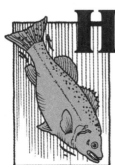

The pizza was made a popular American dish when enthusiastic soldiers returned from Italy after World War II. It evolved probably from early Egyptian flat bread or from the matzohs of the Jews of ancient Israel. Roman soldiers occupying those lands found the flat breads lacked flavor. So they sprinkled herbs and crushed cheese on it, put olive oil atop the cheese, and put it on the hot hearth. That's how pizza was born. Many variations were created in the pizza parlors you now find on almost every block. But how good a food is it? Could you survive by eating only pizzas? Yes, says Dr. Marion Nestle, head of the nutrition department at New York University. If you're stranded on a desert island that happens to have a pizza parlor, she said, you could do a lot worse.

Of course you'd have to eat enough to get the calories, as well as the protein, vitamins, minerals, antioxidants, and other nutrients you need. Not to worry. A real cheese pizza made of yeast dough and covered with real tomato sauce? Not a perfect diet, but you could survive for a very long time. The scientist didn't mention those extra goodies—peppers, onions, Italian sausage, mushrooms, anchovies, pepperoni, fresh basil. Yummmmmm . . .

How fish are farmed

As population pressure increases, the world turns to the oceans for animal protein. Because farmland has become scarcer and scarcer, it's hoped that fish will replace meat. But all 17 of the world's major fisheries are already being fished at or near capacity. Nine are actually in decline. Oceanic fisheries have been pushed to their biological limits.

Take Japan's problem. Its consumption of seafood, about 10 million tons, is one of the largest in the world.

If China—whose population is ten times larger than Japan's—were to become just as dependent on seafood for animal protein, it would need 100 million tons of seafood. Yet the world's total fish harvest in 1994 was exactly that amount—100 million tons.

As the 21st century approaches, many other countries hungry for seafood were sending out fishing fleets in anxious pursuit of it. Unfortunately, there's not enough for everyone. China is one of the nations trying to satisfy the need largely by fish-farming. In the 1990s it was producing some 6 million tons of fish—mostly carp—per year. But note that each ton of fish produced had to be fed two tons of grain. That put more pressure on the country's shrinking grainfields. Result: Grain prices rise, which makes it more costly for fish-farming.

Where human demand presses against the limits of natural fisheries, the loss of food security becomes a global environmental threat. As long as population growth continues, the seafood catch per person will continue to shrink.

You can't separate the prospect of acute scarcity from the issue of distribution. If the food supply isn't expanding, who will get what? How will the smaller pie be divided? When demand outruns supply, prices rise. What happens to the world's poorest people, who cannot afford the price?

The coming crisis has made fish-farming (also called aquaculture) one of the world's fastest-growing food industries. By the mid-1990s at least 20 percent of the seafood catch came from fish farms. It reached nearly 21 million tons, three times the production of a decade earlier.

In the United States, the domestic industry includes shrimp ponds along the Gulf Coast, salmon farms off Maine and Washington, catfish ponds in the southeast, trout farms in Idaho, and the shellfish beds of Connecticut, Louisiana, and Puget Sound.

Most of America's fish-farming is done by small companies. Some fish are raised in small inland ponds in rural areas and then sold live locally or as a frozen product nationwide. People tank-raise rockfish, bass, and catfish in vacant city warehouses and former distilleries. Just as land farming has intensified production by developing better seeds through genetic research, so aquaculture is trying to catch up on the scientific side. Good water quality and the prevention of pollution are prime considerations.

How food processing became industrialized

Giant food-processing industries have created fundamental changes in what Americans produce and consume. Until after the Civil War the food industry relied on small, independent farmers growing and processing their products. Some farmers did the marketing themselves, but more sold what they raised to local middlemen who then sold them in bulk to the food outlets. People in the towns and cities were dependent on store-bought goods. Most groceries were family enterprises. Although the age of the chain store had begun, the chains were still networks of small stores.

By 1914, however, large corporations had begun to dominate all aspects of the food system. They raised huge amounts of investment capital and spent the money on the development of techniques of mass production. Like other major industries, they began to integrate their operations vertically, so that they controlled every stage of production and distribution. Their massive size and their ability to market their products on a national and international scale enabled them to dominate the marketplace.

Heinz, Campbell, Swift, Armour, Borden, Pillsbury, Nabisco, United Fruit—these and other food giants ruled the roost. No longer did the food producers simply respond to what the consumer wanted. Now they used modern advertising and promotion methods to shape the consumer's demands. They mounted large campaigns planned to change food habits by persuasion. On billboards, in newspapers and magazines, over radio and television, by package labels, they influenced the tastes and preferences of the consumer. They persuaded people to try new foods, to switch from one brand to another, to change their diets.

The goal? Not to make and keep people healthy, but rather to increase the corporation's profits (as in any other enterprise). By the 1930s the amount of money invested in food-processing businesses had placed them ahead of such giants as steel and textiles in capital investment.

The companies were battling for the consumer's dollar, but in a limited market. Americans who had the money to buy were getting enough to eat. They couldn't eat more. So to make more money the companies had to convince consumers to buy their products, not the competition's. That required slick promotion campaigns for catchy brand names to distinguish their products from others that were basically the same. Almost anything that worked was allowable, including half truths and false claims. Women and children were the chief targets of promotion.

Professor Brett Silverstein, in a study of the American food production and marketing system, claims that "it is designed to benefit the corporations that run it at the expense of everyone else: consumers, family farmers, small shopkeepers, taxpayers, farmworkers, women, poor people, and citizens of developing nations."

One method the food giants all use is to concentrate their resources. Small companies merge, then the larger ones that result take over other small companies. Big companies are captured by even bigger ones. Beatrice Foods, for example, acquired 400 companies between 1894 and 1984.

The giant firms seek to control as many aspects of their business as possible. They mechanize farming and processing to reduce the labor force and control the workers. They make research grants to control the food technology that is developed. They lobby and make election campaign contributions to control government decisions. They use advertising and marketing campaigns to control consumer choice. And they manipulate genetics to control the biological makeup of crops. All done in the quest for profits.

███

How chickens and hogs are mass-produced

They call it "agribusiness."

By that is meant farming by giant corporations using modern industrial methods for mass production of food.

The chicken business is an example.

Up until the 1920s chickens were raised mostly on farms, with the housewife and children looking after the flock. On average, each farm had about two dozen birds. The chickens lived an outdoor life, roaming the yard for food during the day, sheltering in the stables or sheds in chicken coops in winter. Farmers used some chickens for food and sold some and their eggs locally.

But soon hatcheries with artificial incubators and brooders became common. Genetic research laboratories developed ways to breed chickens for such economic values as heavy egg laying. Both feed and pharmaceutical companies entered a growing and profitable industry. They recognized that a rapidly increasing population would create a demand for cheap, mass-produced poultry and eggs.

The chickens are divided into two genetic types—broiler chickens for meat production and laying hens for egg production. And these are now grown in what amounts to chicken and egg factories. Huge numbers of laying hens are kept in small wire battery cages, stacked in rows and tiers in long buildings holding 50,000 to 125,000 hens. The space in a cage doesn't allow them to stand still in a normal way. Forced into a cramped position for their short life, the birds suffer disease. The broiler chickens are kept in confinement sheds. This form of factory farming has been called "concentration camps for chickens" by people who have worked in them or have visited them.

As many as 100 million laying chicks a week are grown in this way. They live indoors and are fed through automatic conveyer belts. Their manure drops on other belts, which deposit it in large pits. To spur growth, artificial light simulates longer days. The chickens are plucked by machines. Electric heaters and fans keep the birds warm in winter and cool in summer.

The food corporations control poultry raising by signing chicken farmers to contracts that specify the number of birds to be raised, at set conditions, and set prices. To keep their farms going the farmers accept capital from the corporation and agree to the terms demanded. If they don't, they are likely to lose their farms in the face of competition from chicken factories.

To make production on a large scale quick and profitable, drugs are used to promote fast growth and combat the diseases that thrive in crowded confinement. Feed additives, fungicides, and pesticides all play a chemical role in the chicken factory because natural processes move too slowly for quick profits.

Much the same industrialized approach is used on pig farms. A British TV documentary shown in March 1997 was based on secret filming by a reporter who took a job as a pig man. The film revealed factory farming where piglets are crushed to death by their mothers because their pens are so cramped, especially since pigs are now bred to gross size. Sick pigs, illegally, are sometimes not separated in "poorly" pens. Tails are cut off without anesthetics and, illegally, not by a vet. Much of the disease and death he observed, said the reporter, "is due to stress and their being crowded so close together." The factory farms are compared to the appalling slums of huge cities.

An American documentary televised in the summer of 1997 covered a similar story, in its portrait of conditions in North Carolina pig factories, where ten million pigs a year are raised.

The industrial system of growing animals is applied to crops as well. In traditional farming, crop rotation, the use of manure as fertilizer, and the planting of alternate rows with different crops provide nutrients to the soil, producing healthy food while protecting the land. But the corporate system ignores the classic model. It seeks the maximum amount of cropland on which to use the latest industrial methods. Massive amounts of synthetic fertilizers are applied to replace crop rotation. Enormous amounts of pesticides too are used to kill insects, weeds, and fungi. They also kill other organisms—birds, bees, ducks, pelicans. And what about the damage to the people who do the farm labor? And the consumers who eat the food?

Some pesticides are banned, heavily restricted, or have never been registered in the United States, yet they are allowed to be exported, and when applied on the farms of unsuspecting countries they do great damage. Not only are consumers abroad at great risk for pesticide poisoning, but in buying imported food Americans risk harm from pesticides that were originally banned here.

How teenagers eat

"The growing American teenager eats 1,817 pounds (824 kilograms) of food in a single year. This is equivalent in weight to a total of 474 Big Macs, 349 Whoppers with cheese, 286 frozen pizzas, 726 hot dogs, 210 peanut butter-and-jelly sandwiches, 159 banana splits, 600 doughnuts, 200 boxes of Cap'n Crunch cereal, 1,271 chocolate sandwich cookies, 340 Twinkies, 188 packages of M&M's, 690 Hershey bars, 129 Fudgsicles, 47 gallons (178 liters) of chocolate ice cream, 1,178 Reese's peanut butter cups, and one serving of home-cooked meat loaf, mashed potatoes, and spinach."

—from *Prevention's Giant Book of Health Facts.*

How safe is our food?

The safety of America's food supply has become a serious problem. A 1997 report by the Center for Science in the Public Interest said that "every year food poisoning kills approximately 9,000 Americans. And that figure may be the tip of the iceberg because of underreporting. Another 33 million become ill annually from food poisoning." The Food and Drug Administration (FDA) admits that microbiological hazards represent the biggest problem in our food supply. Many people suffer from contaminated meat, poultry, seafood, and other foods.

A major cause of the trouble is the small budget of the FDA's program to keep food free from dangerous microbes, food additives, and contaminants. Responsibility for protecting the public's health is scattered among four different federal agencies. Their food safety functions ought to be combined into one well-funded federal food agency as the least expensive and most effective way to safeguard the nation's food supply. In an ideal world there would also be a single agency monitoring foreign countries to make sure they are enforcing tougher standards.

The foods most likely to contain pesticides are fruits and vegetables. About half those tested have pesticide residues in them. Grains—wheat and bread—tend not to have residues because milling often removes them. Meat and dairy products are a problem only in certain cases. Since some pesticides tend to accumulate in fat, fatty meats, fish, and dairy products may have higher residue levels than lean or low-fat animal products.

A reasonably diverse diet is the way to lessen the chance of exposure to pesticides. The more kinds of food you eat, the less your exposure to any given pesticide. Properly washing and peeling fruits and vegetables helps a lot.

If people bought fresh and processed organic foods it would help them to avoid pesticides. Tests show that organic foods usually contain no detectable pesticide residues. Congress several years ago authorized a National Organic Program that proposes a uniform definition of "organic" and would set up a nationwide system to certify producers and processors.

How cooking made us more fully human

Cooking is simply the process of using heat to prepare food for eating. If one were to try to trace the history of cooking in any detail, it would get more and more complicated. The first humans to inhabit the Earth lived on what they could gather in the fields and woods and streams, or what they could hunt. That food was unrefined, but it gave strength and health. It built the body and extended its life. When farming began it added much variety to food.

Eating is the most natural activity. (You couldn't survive unless you did it.) For hundreds of thousands of years people ate their food raw. When fire was first deliberately used, cooking was discovered. There are many theories or guesses as to when and where that happened. The only certainty is that it must have been a very long time ago, possibly in Africa, possibly in Asia.

Did cooking food make it taste better? Very likely. For heat helps release protein and carbohydrates as well as break down fiber. That increases the nutritional value of many foods. And it makes it possible for us to eat some foods that would otherwise be inedible. Which, in turn must have improved health. One anthropologist, Carleton Coon, even claims that cooking was "the decisive factor in leading man from a primarily animal existence into one that was more fully human."

A story by the English writer Charles Lamb suggests how people first experienced the joy cooking provides. A Chinese peasant's hut, in which a litter of pigs was kept, caught fire from some stray sparks. As the building burned down, a strange and delectable smell rose from the ashes. And lo, roast pork was discovered.

Something like this may well have happened thousands of years earlier, when a piece of meat a hunter had brought home fell into the campfire and had to be left there till the flames died out. That family enjoyed its first sizzling steak. Cooking was refined when someone figured out that the meat would not shrink so much if it was cooked more slowly over embers or on a flat stone by the side of the fire.

Improvements came as people learned that wrapping big leaves around the meat protected it from the flames, or that cutting up meat and roasting the pieces on a spit would cook it faster than if it were in one big chunk.

The use of ovens may go back to 25,000 B.C. In the Ukraine, excavations revealed several quite small pits dug in the earth around a hearth—probably food ovens in which leaf-wrapped food was cooked on a bed of hot embers.

Boiling food was probably done too in larger pits lined with flat stones to prevent seepage. Water was poured in over stones heated in the campfire, the food was added, and while it was cooking, more hot stones were slid in to keep the temperature up. In some places cooking was done in large mollusk or reptile shells. One naturalist reported eating a delicious soup that was made from the entrails of a turtle, chopped up and boiled in the concave upper shell of the creature.

In Central America, around 7000 B.C., people were using stone cooking pots. These were so heavy they were placed in the center of the hearth and kept there. The Greek historian Herodotus tells us that in the fifth century B.C. the nomad Scythians put all of an animal's flesh into its stomach bag, mixed water with it, and boiled it over the fire. In that way an ox, for instance, was ingeniously made to cook itself, he said. Of course improved leather-working techniques made it possible to replace such older containers with animal skins. Then came pottery, followed by bronze and next iron, the metal commonly used until the 20th century.

When Rome's power was at its height, the chefs of the rich sharpened their masters' appetite by the number and diversity of the dishes they served. They were so skilled they could change the appearance of any item they prepared. If their master wanted a kind of fish that was not available in that season or climate, they were able to make other fish taste and look like the one they couldn't get at the market. For Romans less well off, cooking was simply the preparation of food to satisfy the elementary needs of life.

Some historians of cooking view this as an example of the moral contrast between a simple, natural way of cooking and an artificial art by which all sorts of tricks are used to disguise natural foodstuffs to indulge corrupt tastes. Others, however, see the history of cooking as a kind of progress. As the cook's practical knowledge increases, through it new pleasures are found.

■ ■ ■

How to cook up a storm

Advice on what to eat and how to cook it has long been handed out by gifted amateurs and professional cooks. As far back as the fifth century B.C., when Athens was a center of art and culture, at least a dozen books on the art of cooking were available. One Greek expert roamed "all lands and seas," he said, in his desire to "test carefully the delights of the belly." Among the delicacies he prized were a pig that had died of overeating and the eggs of the peacock.

We know something about the eating habits of the Roman aristocracy in the first century A.D. from a fictional book by Petronius called *The Satyricon*. The feast he describes was only for the wealthy, with a great many slaves required to produce it. The Roman gourmet Apicius gathered a large number of recipes, which were not published till long after his death. He is said to have poisoned himself when he realized he no longer had enough money to maintain his high standard of living.

Cookbooks in France were directed to the aristocracy alone until the rise of the middle class opened up that market. In 1739, François Marin put out the first cookbook for the ordinary family. In 1746 the French writer Menon published a hugely popular 400-page cookbook for those "third-class" persons with suggestions for how to eat well but cheaply. Until then housewives had learned only from local tradition. In the early 1800s, Louis Audot (men reigned supreme as chefs in France) issued a book for the "modest" household, which, by the end of the century, had gone through 79 editions. The trouble with many of these books was that they reproduced recipes beyond the capacity of the average kitchen or cook.

English cooking has suffered the reputation of being about the worst there is. But that couldn't be for lack of cookbooks. The first one appeared in 1500. In 1615 (the year before Shakespeare's death), Gervase Markham published *The English House-wife*; it proved profitable through eight editions. Many of these how-to books taught the housewife not only how to prepare and serve meals but how to instruct the servants, keep the accounts, weave, sew, brew, and cure. The most successful was Hannah Glasse's *The Art of Cooking Made Plain and Easy*, which even dared to borrow French recipes. Queen Victoria's chief cook, Charles Edme Francatell, reached beyond the royal household to let all classes know how to prepare sheep's jowls and ears as well as reindeer tongues. His *The Modern Cook* was published in 1845.

In the United States, the use of cookbooks spread as literacy increased. Far more women by the early 19th century were able to read them. One of the early efforts was made by Lydia Maria Child, a young New Englander, daughter of a baker, who had begun a brilliant career as a novelist, taken up the unpopular cause of abolitionism, founded the first children's magazine, and now ventured a book on "good housekeeping." Married to a lawyer whose advocacy of social reforms brought little income, Maria had to learn how to make do with very little. She had to be creative. Thinking of all the housewives who shared her problem, with her usual directness she soon produced *The Frugal Housewife*. In its first year, 1830, it sold 6,000 copies, a lot for that time, and five years later, 14 editions had been published. For years it was one of the most popular and valued books in American households. Abroad, it went through many editions in England, Scotland, and Germany.

A cookbook—and something more—it was dedicated "To Those Who Are Not Ashamed of Economy." She claimed that if a family followed her advice, it could live on $600 a year. Nothing expensive was in her recipes. All were helpful and useful (although one of her cakes required 3 pounds of butter and 28 eggs).

She listed what cuts of meat to buy and advised buying them in quantity, told how to dry-cure, urged baking one's own bread and cakes. There were recipes for beer and wine too. Sprinkled among the recipes were brief essays on economy. Her book was a success because all those that had preceded it had been written for the wealthy. The families of workers and farmers badly needed what she had to say as they struggled to make ends meet.

One of the most popular cookbooks in American history—the *Boston Cooking School Cook Book*—appeared in 1896. Written by Fanny Farmer, it warned against those miserable people who live to eat. To be truly educated, she said, you must know the principles of diet. Then you'll "eat to live, do better mental and physical work, and disease will be less frequent."

Most of Fanny Farmer's menus for family luncheons and dinners were quite simple. Soup, meat or fish, potatoes, two vegetables, dessert, cheese, and coffee. Gradually menus for the best diet shifted toward smaller and less elaborate meals.

The book most people probably know best today is *The Joy of Cooking*. It was created in the early days of the Great Depression by Irma Rombauer, of a German-American family in St. Louis. She published the first edition herself in 1931, depending on friends and relatives for many of the recipes. She had no patience with elaborate "gourmet" cookbooks which made a big deal out of "artistic" food preparation. Nor did she prefer any country's cuisine over another's. She made room for the most diverse foods, seeing them all as "equals in the republic of taste."

A commercial publisher took up the *Joy of Cooking*, which was now coauthored with Irma's daughter, Marion Rombauer Becker. It was a best-seller, year after year, in its field. The current edition is edited by Marion's son Ethan Becker and features contributions by many prominent food writers.

Nowadays, it seems, cookbooks are replacing cooks in very many homes.

How burgers and fatness go together

Is the American waistline getting fatter? And the arteries thicker?

It seems so. The number of overweight people held steady at one out of four in the 1960s and 1970s. But in the 1980s it shot up to one out of three, according to the Federal Center for Disease Control and Prevention in Atlanta. (To be medically obese is to be more than 25 percent above ideal weight.)

Hamburgers share some of the blame for fatness. They are the worst food in the average American diet. They contribute more artery-clogging fat than any other single food. This is the claim of the Center for Science in the Public Interest. The burgers are a nutritionist's nightmare, for as prices at the fast-food places go down, the amount of fat in the American diet goes up. Yet research shows that you can't just blame the fast-food business, for people who eat high-fat foods in restaurants also eat high-fat foods at home.

America's appetite for take-out junk food is insatiable. Hamburgers, french fries, and chicken nuggets are among the five fastest-growing foods ordered in restaurants, a consumer study shows. Some happy eaters, however, claim that Americans are obsessed with thinness. Let's have a new beauty aesthetic, they say, one based on the increasing plumpness of the population.

Americans live in the most health- and diet-obsessed culture in the world. About 40 percent of women and 15 percent of men are on a diet at any given time. But within five years of beginning a diet, 95 percent of all dieters are fatter than they were when they began.

Maybe by telling people fat is bad for them and encouraging them to diet, something within us is triggered that results in our getting fatter. Does it all go back to our genetic inheritance? In prehistoric times, the hunter-gatherer stage, we were programmed to eat as much as we could because we had to exercise all day, scrounging for seeds and berries in the woods, hunting mammoths, starting fires, running from animal and human danger. Fatness would have been very rare in such a time. Now, when most of us are sedentary, our balance of calorie-intake and expenditure is off. We keep eating more than we need, perhaps because that's the way we are.

How we went from Babylon's cookshops to McDonald's

Buying ready-cooked food to take home is an ancient custom. Back in the sixth century B.C., when Nebuchadrezzar ruled ancient Babylonia, people were going to cookshops to buy prepared meals. It might be roast mutton, fish, fritters, pancakes, or sweetmeats.

In the Rome of the Caesars, working-class families avoided preparing meals at home if they could. Their kitchen equipment was poor, fuel was hard to get, and fire a constant hazard in the tall jam-packed tenements that lined the streets. So they bought their food at the cookshops that cluttered the neighborhood. It could be salt fish or goat cheese or a slice of roast pork, and maybe olives or figs to go with it.

The Chinese too had cookshops, more advanced and varied than anywhere else. Because of China's great diversity of climate and vegetation and its regionally separate cultures, there were many variations in diet. It was different for the rich whose homes were equipped to produce the wide range of foods required for even a modest feast. But many of the people ate out, as Marco Polo observed on his visit to China in the 13th century. In taverns, hotels, teahouses, noodle shops, each cook prepared his own specialties—barbecued meats, steamed pork buns, won ton, chilled fruits, honey fritters, fish soups.

When Friar Odoric visited China a century later, he learned that when a man wanted to give a dinner for his friends, he went to a hostel and ordered exactly what he wanted for a fixed price. If a wealthy man was showing off, he would provide a supper that included a dozen soups, some 40 dishes of boiled, stewed, stir-fried, steamed, roasted, or barbecued meat, poultry, and seafood. Plus a great variety of vegetables, fruits, rice dishes, and fish. And finally, drinks to cool the palate and revive the appetite between courses.

If you think such a Chinese meal was beyond what anyone could absorb, remember the famous American glutton, Diamond Jim Brady. He began work as a bellhop and ended as a wealthy financier. His gargantuan appetite was a legend in the New York of the 1890s. "Jim Brady is the best 25 customers we have," said the owner of Rector's, a favorite restaurant. When the first American-made Sole Marguery was served to Brady, he devoured nine orders of it before easing on to the next course. A normal dinner for him might be two dozen oysters, half a dozen crabs, two bowls of turtle soup, six or seven lobsters followed by two ducks, a large sirloin steak with vegetables, and a full tray of French pastries. After the meal, chatting with his friends, he would pop into his mouth, one after the other, all the chocolates in a 2-pound (0.9 kilogram) box.

Anyone else might have needed 24 hours to recover from such a feast, but Brady ate six meals a day. Once, celebrating the victory of one of his racehorses, he gave a dinner for 50 guests. The feast began at 4:00 P.M. and did not end until 9:00 the next morning. The bill? $100,000.

In Brady's time, people who lived at the opposite end of the economic scale ate very differently. Factory workers often grabbed a quick bite at horse-drawn lunch carts that prowled industrial districts. Then, in the early 1920s, diners appeared. At first they were adapted from abandoned railway dining cars. The menu featured chili, hamburgers, french fries, soup, pie, and coffee.

As American incomes rose and families began dining out together now and then, roadside diners sprang up, adding special kiddie menus and lighter meals, including salads, to the menu. By 1950 there were some 6,000 prefabricated diners sprinkled around the country. The majority of diner customers were immigrants or second-generation Americans—German, Irish, Italian, Jewish. Some diner cooks prepared European meals for their ethnic customers but also dished out standard American items: beef stew, franks and beans, roast turkey, chipped beef on toast, and pie and coffee.

Restaurant patrons were rapidly increasing. People were eating away from home more than ever before—some because they had more money to spend, others because women by the millions had entered the full-time workforce and had little time for cooking.

But nothing remains the same. New types of eating places competed with the old diners: family restaurant chains, coffee shops, drive-ins, and ultimately, the fast-food outlets. The national chains stressed fast service, rock-bottom prices, informality, and attention to family needs. They standardized food and service as well as architectural design.

McDonald's, Kentucky Fried Chicken, Burger King, Denny's, Pizza Hut, Taco Bell, Wendy's, Hardee's, Starbucks, and dozens of other chains jumped into the crowded business. They use assembly-line production methods developed by industry. By the 1990s surveys showed that every third meal was taken in some sort of eating place, and not at home.

In the United States in the 1990s there were over 350,000 eating places, with a total sale of $160 billion. All this doesn't mean that entering the restaurant business is a safe investment. For the life of a restaurant can be extremely short. Of 3,000 eating places opening in New York City each year, nearly 2,000 fail within a year.

How many people can the Earth support?

When agriculture rose 10,000 years ago, the population of the globe was about 4 million. The world's population is now growing by that amount every ten days. By the time the 21st century begins, there will be more than 6 billion people on the planet, up 3.5 billion just since 1950. If population growth continues at the present rate, there will be 12 billion people by the year 2050.

How many people can the Earth support?

Since 1968 an estimated 200 million people, most of them children, have died of hunger and diseases related to malnutrition. One billion go hungry every day. If the food supply is not enough to take care of everyone now, what does that mean for a population that will be twice as large 50 years from now?

Scientists who study both agriculture and ecology predict a grim future. Cropland—those land areas covered with soil in which crops can be grown—is not unlimited. A scientific study concludes that "only about 3.2 billion hectares of the total 13 billion hectares of the Earth's ice-free land surface can be cultivated." Most of it is already under cultivation, and much prime farmland is now being degraded or lost. Land, water, energy, are being used up rapidly. So fast that for a population of 12 billion there will be worldwide "absolute misery, poverty, disease, starvation." There are just not enough resources for 12 billion people in the future to live as Americans do today. Depletion of the fossil fuels—coal, oil, natural gas—are one factor limiting the number of people able to thrive on Earth. Two other major limiting factors are cropland and fresh water. These scientists call for a reduction in population growth, to 1.5 children per family. Some governments have been able to slow the rate of population growth. The policies that have been effective include quality education for girls, economic security for women, and access to family planning.

Other experts hold that improvements in agriculture will provide the increase in food necessary to sustain the population predicted for the year 2050. The pessimists say okay, hope for the best but plan for the worst.

In any case, the answer to the question, "How many people can the Earth support?" requires more than simple arithmetic. It is limited by the facts of nature. Among these are constraints on food, water, energy, land, soil, space, diseases, waste disposal, nonfuel minerals, forests, biological diversity, biologically accessible nitrogen, phosphorus, climatic change. And, equally important, by the important role of choices people make.

AFTERWORD

So whatever else we do, we eat.

Because we have to, if we're to go on living.

And because we like to.

But what we eat, and how we eat, is tied to the way we live, as this book tries to demonstrate.

As part of daily life, food expresses a people's customs. Wheat? Rice? Tea? Chocolate? Meat? Fish? Potatoes? Who eats them and why? Look carefully at a people's eating habits and you come to a better understanding of the diversity of human life. Sometimes food may reveal more than the study of great historical events or the deeds of kings and generals.

Foodways constantly change and evolve, of course. The birth of farming, the rise of cities, the spread of industry, the invasion of countries, and countless other factors shape what we put in our mouths. Some food customs persist for centuries. Others die quickly.

One aspect of the story we could not ignore is the link between food and power. Control of the food supply—that is a primary instrument of power for any governing group, as this book demonstrates. Eating habits may even become a moral issue. (To eat meat or not eat meat?)

As James Yood writes in a book celebrating food in art: "First we cry, then we eat. And eat and eat and eat; from birth until death, this fundamental activity continues. . . . Eating is intertwined with almost every aspect of our existence."

SELECTED BIBLIOGRAPHY

Anderson, E.N. *The Food of China*. New Haven: Yale University, 1988.

Bailey, Ronald, ed. *The True State of the Planet*. New York: Free Press, 1995.

Barber, Benjamin R. *Jihad vs. McWorld*. New York: Times, 1995.

Becker, Jasper. *Hungry Ghosts: Mao's Secret Famine*. New York: Free Press, 1997.

Braudel, Fernand. *Capitalism and Material Life 1400–1800*. New York: Harper & Row, 1973.

————. *The Mediterranean*. New York: Harper & Row, 1972.

Brown, Lester R. *Who Will Feed China?* New York: Norton, 1995.

Brown, Lester R., et al. *State of the World*. New York: Norton, 1997.

Cartwright, Frederick E., and Michael D. Biddiss. *Disease and History*. New York: Dorset, 1972.

Childe, Gordon. *What Happened in History*. New York: Penguin, 1942.

Cohen, Joel E. *How Many People Can the Earth Support?* New York: Norton, 1995.

Cohen, Mark Nathan. *Health and the Rise of Civilization*. New Haven: Yale University, 1989.

Commoner, Barry. *Making Peace With the Planet*. New York: Pantheon, 1990.

Curwen, E.C. *Plough and Pasture*. London: Cobbett, 1946.

Davis, Karen. *Prisoned Chickens, Poisoned Eggs*. Summertown, Tenn: Book Publishing Co., 1996.

Diamond, Jared. *Guns, Germs and Steel*. New York: Norton, 1997.

Dunne, Lavon J. *Nutrition Almanac*. New York: McGraw Hill, 1990.

Ehrlich, Paul R. and Anne H. Ehrlich. *Healing the Planet*. Reading, Mass.: Addison-Wesley, 1991.

Elkort, Martin. *The Secret Life of Food*. Los Angeles: Tarcher, 1991.

Figes, Orlando. *A People's Tragedy: A History of the Russian Revolution*. New York: Viking, 1997.

Flants, Musya and Joyce Toomre, eds. *Food in Russian History and Culture*. Bloomington: Indiana University, 1997.

Forster, Robert and Orest Ranum, eds. *Food and Drink in History*. Baltimore: Johns Hopkins, 1979.

Herbst, Sharon Tyler. *The Food Lover's Companion*. Hauppage, N.Y.: Barron's, 1990.

Hillel, Daniel. *Out of the Earth*. Berkeley: University of California, 1991.

Kinealy, Christine. *A Death-Dealing Famine: The Great Hunger in Ireland*. Pluto, London, 1997.

Kurten, Bjorn. *Our Earliest Ancestors*. New York: Columbia, 1993.

Larkin, Jack. *The Reshaping of Everyday Life, 1796–1840*. New York: Harper & Row, 1988.

Levenstein, Harvey. *Paradox of Plenty: A Social History of Eating in Modern America*. New York: Oxford, 1993.

————. *Revolution at the Table: The Transformation of the American Diet*. New York: Oxford, 1988.

Lopez, Robert S. *The Birth of Europe*. New York: M. Evans, 1967.

Okakura, Kazuko. *The Book of Tea*. Boston: Shambala, 1993.

Pool, Daniel. *What Jane Austen Ate and Charles Dickens Knew*. New York: Touchstone, 1993.

Raeburn, Paul. *The Last Harvest*. Lincoln, Neb.: University of Nebraska, 1995.

Rifkin, Jeremy. *Beyond Beef: The Rise and Fall of the Cattle Culture*. New York: Plume, 1992.

Root, Waverly and Richard De Rochemont. *Eating in America*. New York: Ecco, 1995.

Silverstein, Brett. *Fed Up! The Food Forces that Make You Fat, Sick and Poor*. Boston: South End, 1984.

Tannahill, Reay. *Food in History*. New York: Crown, 1988.

Unger, Sanford J. *Africa: The People and Politics of an Emerging Continent.* New York: Touchstone, 1989.

Wolf, Eric R. *Europe and the People Without History.* Berkeley: University of California, 1982.

Zeldin, Theodore. *An Intimate History of Humanity.* New York: HarperCollins, 1994.

▌INDEX▐

▍ABOUT THE AUTHOR▍

Milton Meltzer has published more than ninety books for young people and adults in the fields of history and biography. His life of Langston Hughes, a National Book Award finalist, was issued by Millbrook Press in a new illustrated edition in 1997. He has dealt with such diverse topics as weapons and warfare, slavery, piracy, memory, names, the potato, gold, and the horse. He has written or edited for newspapers, magazines, books, radio, television, and films.

Among the many honors for his books are five nominations for the National Book Award as well as the Christopher, Jane Addams, Carter G. Woodson, Jefferson Cup, Washington Book Guild, Olive Branch, and Golden Kite awards. Many of his books have been chosen for the honor lists of the American Library Association, the National Council of Teachers of English, the National Council for the Social Studies, as well as *The New York Times* Best Books of the Year list.

Meltzer and his wife, Hildy, live in New York City. They have two daughters, Jane and Amy, and two grandsons, Benjamin and Zachary. Mr. Meltzer is a member of the Authors Guild, American PEN, and the Organization of American Historians.